MATH GIRLS

TALK ABOUT

TRIGONOMETRY

Fundamental Skills for Advanced Mathematics

BY HIROSHI YUKI

Author of MATH GIRLS

TRANSLATED BY TONY GONZALEZ

MATH GIRLS TALK ABOUT TRIGONOMETRY

Originally published as *Sūgaku Gāru No Himitsu Nōto Marui Sankaku Kansū*
Copyright © 2014 Hiroshi Yuki
Softbank Creative Corp., Tokyo

English translation © 2014 by Tony Gonzalez
Edited by Joseph Reeder and M.D. Hendon
Cover design by Kasia Bytnerowicz

Published 2014 by

Bento Books, Inc.
Austin, Texas 78732

bentobooks.com

ISBN 978-1-939326-26-3 (hardcover)
ISBN 978-1-939326-25-6 (trade paperback)
Library of Congress Control Number: 2014958329

Printed in the United States of America
First edition, December 2014

Math Girls Talk About
Trigonometry

To My Readers

This book is a collection of conversations between Miruka, Tetra, Yuri, and our narrator.

If there are places where you don't understand what they're talking about, or equations you don't understand, feel free to skip over those parts. But please do your best to keep up with them.

That's the best way to make yourself part of the conversation.

—Hiroshi Yuki

Cast of Characters

I am your narrator. I'm a junior in high school, and I love math. Equations in particular.

Miruka is my age. She's so good at math, it's scary. She has long black hair and wears metal frame glasses.

Tetra is one year younger than me, and a bundle of energy. She cuts her hair short and has big, beautiful eyes.

Yuri is my cousin, an eighth grader. She has a chestnut ponytail and excels at logic.

Ms. Mizutani is our school librarian.

Mom is, well, just my mom.

Contents

Prologue

We look at shapes, and think we can see them. We see triangles as triangles, circles as circles. Anyone can see a shape. They're right there, plain as day—or are they? Might there be circles hiding in triangles? Triangles in circles?

Join us as we search for shapes that cannot be seen, for shapes hiding in other forms. We'll find new ways of looking at things, ways of broadening our vision to see that which cannot be seen. We'll start with triangles, and find the circles hiding in them. In those circles, we'll discover lurking spirals. We'll start with questions, and find equations hiding in them. In those equations, we'll discover a new world.

Come with us. Together we'll create new shapes, ones that only we can see.

CHAPTER 1

Round Triangles

"Names describe forms. Forms
represent essence."

1.1 STARTING THE JOURNEY

In the library after school one day, I found Tetra furiously scribbling
equations in her notebook.

Me	"Hey, Tetra. Doing some math?"
Tetra	"Yeah. I never thought it would happen, but after start-ing to study with you guys, I'm actually learning to like this stuff!"
Me	"So what are you working on now?"
Tetra	"Something completely new! Trigonometry!"
Me	"Sines and cosines and all that, huh."
Tetra	"Yeah..."

Tetra's face darkens.

Me	"What's wrong?"
Tetra	"Well, I was hoping this would give me more fun things to talk about with you and Miruka, but it's harder than I expected."
Me	"It can be confusing at first, but it's not so bad once you get used to it."
Tetra	"At first I thought it was just about playing with triangles, but it looks like there's all kinds of other stuff too. Just what *is* trigonometry?"
Me	"I don't think there's a simple answer to that. How about we talk about it some, and see what we find?"
Tetra	"That would be great!"

1.2 RIGHT TRIANGLES

Me	"I don't know how deep you've gotten so far, so I'll start with the absolute basics."
Tetra	"Perfect."
Me	"Okay, start by drawing a right triangle."
Tetra	"Like this?"

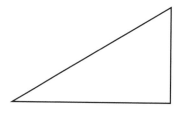

Me	"Well, that *looks* like a right triangle..."

Tetra   "Did I do something wrong?"

Me   "When you draw a right triangle, it's best to put a box on the right angle."

Tetra   "Oh, I've seen that! Like this, right?"

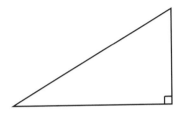

A right triangle with the right angle indicated

Me   "Exactly. That makes sure the reader knows what you're trying to show."

Tetra   "Got it."

Tetra pulls out her "secret notebook" and makes a quick note.

1.3 Naming Angles

Me   "Some more basics. A triangle has three angles, and in a right triangle one of those angles is 90°."

Tetra   "That's the right angle that makes right triangles right. Right?"

Me   "Uh...correct. So, anyway, there are two other angles. We're going to name one of them theta."

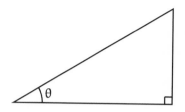

We name one of the angles θ

Tetra	"Theta... That's how you read this Greek letter?"
Me	"It is. Angles are often named using Greek letters. That's just a convention, though. We don't have to name them like that, if you don't want to."
Tetra	"No, that's fine. Let's go with the Greek."
Me	"Just checking. Math uses lots of symbols to name things, and I know that puts some people off."
Tetra	"Well, to be honest I still get a little freaked out when there's a whole bunch of them. It starts to feel like it's all too much to digest."
Me	"Everybody feels that way at first. Just take it all in at your own pace, and you'll be fine."
Tetra	"I dunno... My pace can be pretty slow."
Me	"That's okay, the problem isn't going anywhere. It's better to go slow, making sure you get everything, than to race through a bunch of stuff you don't understand. Take time to get to know each symbol, and become friends with it."
Tetra	"I guess if I'm going to master trig, I'll be making a lot of Greek friends!"

Tetra's eyes widens as she smiles.

1.4 NAMING VERTICES AND SIDES

Me   "Since we're naming things, let's name the vertices and
       sides of this triangle, too."

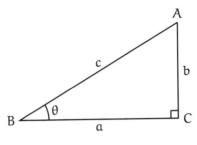

Triangle ABC

Tetra   "So you named the vertices A, B, and C, right?"

Me   "Using capital letters, which is another convention. We
        can string those letters together and call the triangle as
        a whole $\triangle ABC$. You usually label parts of a triangle in
        counter-clockwise order, but—"

Tetra   "—but that's just another convention, so you don't *have*
        to, right?"

Me   "Exactly. But there's one rule you've gotta stick to:
        when you write about a shape, be sure to use the same
        names that are in the diagrams."

Tetra   "Meaning?"

Me   "Like if you write something about $\triangle ABC$, be absolutely
        sure the vertices of that triangle are labelled A, B, C in
        any diagrams."

Tetra   "Got it. Here's A, here's B, and here's C. Looks good!"

Me   "When you name sides, you'll usually use lowercase let-
        ters. That makes it easier to distinguish between sides
        and vertices."

Tetra   "Oh, okay."

Me   "Also, you normally use the lowercase version of the let-
          ter you used to name the vertex that's across from the
          side you're naming."

Tetra   "So we have side lowercase-a across from vertex
          uppercase-A."

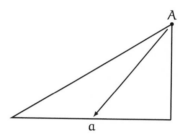

**Name sides using the lowercase version of the letter used
to name their opposite vertices**

Me   "And side lowercase-b across from vertex uppercase-B—"

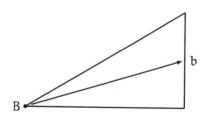

Tetra   "—and side lowercase-c across from vertex uppercase-C."

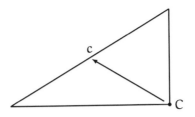

Me "One thing to be careful about: when you want to talk about the *length* of a side, sometimes it's clearer to use the names of that side's vertices with a bar over them. So if I write this..."

$$\overline{AB}$$

Me "...that means 'the length of the side formed by vertices A and B.'"

Tetra "So a lowercase letter is the name of a side, and a pair of vertices with a line over them is the length of a side."

Me "Right. Again, you don't *have* to do things this way. The math will all work the same, no matter what you name things. But this is how people have been doing it for a while now, so unless you have a good reason to do things differently your math will be more legible if you follow their lead."

Tetra "Gotcha!"

1.5 THE SINE FUNCTION

Me "Let's take a closer look at $\angle\theta$ and the sides b and c in this triangle."

Tetra "Okay."

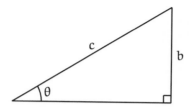

Tetra takes me literally, leaning in to take a closer look at the diagram. She points at the angle and sides, and I hear her muttering their names.

Me   "We want to think about the relationship between the size of $\angle\theta$ and the length of those sides."

Tetra   "They're related?"

Me   "Sure. Think about what would happen if you made side c longer, *without changing the angle of* θ. For example, if we made side c twice as long, our right triangle would look like this."

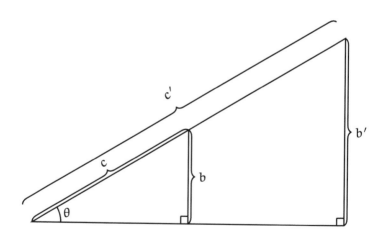

Tetra   "Side c′ is the doubled side c, right?"

Me	"It is. And if we want to do that to side c and still have a right triangle, then we need to stretch side b, too. Side b′ here is that stretched side b."
Tetra	"Makes sense."
Me	"In fact, if we want to double the length of side b, we have to double the length of side c as well. And if we triple one we have to triple the other, and so on."
Tetra	"So the length of sides b and c are in proportion."
Me	"Exactly! In other words, if the measure of $\angle\theta$ remains constant, then the ratio of sides b and c must be a constant, too."
Tetra	"A constant ratio ...?"
Me	"Put another way, if $\angle\theta$ remains constant, then the value of the fraction $\frac{b}{c}$ remains constant."
Tetra	"So like if you double or triple the c in the denominator, you have to double or triple the b in the numerator, too."
Me	"That's right."
Tetra	"Okay, I get that. But this all sounds more like geometry. Does it have anything to do with trigonometry?"
Me	"This *is* trigonometry."
Tetra	"Huh?"
Me	"Look at it this way. Here's what we've been saying."

If the measure of an angle $\angle\theta$ in a right triangle is constant, then the value of the fraction $\frac{b}{c}$ is constant, too.

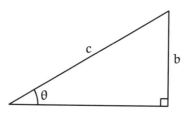

Tetra   "Sure, I get that."

Me   "But here's another way to look at it."

Determining the measure of an angle $\angle\theta$ in a right triangle also determines the value of the fraction $\frac{b}{c}$.

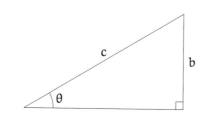

Tetra   "Let me make sure I've got this straight. We want θ to be a certain angle, and we want the triangle to be a right triangle. Side lengths b and c are proportional, which means their ratio is some constant value. So when we set θ to some value, that determines what the value of $\frac{b}{c}$ will be."

Me   "An excellent summary."

Tetra   "Good. I'm not sure how you would find the angle, but
           I see how setting θ to something would set the value of
           $\frac{b}{c}$, too."

Me   "Then how about we give a name to that value of $\frac{b}{c}$ that
           you get from setting θ. Turns out there's already a very
           good one, so we'll use that and call it $\sin \theta$."

           Tetra's eyes widen, and she grabs my arm.

Tetra   "Sine!? Did you just say sine, like the trig function sine?
           That's all it is?"

Me   "What do you mean, 'that's all'?"

Tetra   "You're saying that $\sin \theta$ is just the value of this ratio
           $\frac{b}{c}$?"

Me   "That's all it is. Well, let me take that back. So far we've
           only defined it using right triangles, so that's all it is for
           a θ in the range $0° < \theta < 90°$. But it's correct to say
           that $\sin \theta$ is equal to the value of this ratio $\frac{b}{c}$."

Definition of $\sin \theta$ as a ratio of two sides in a right triangle
$$(0° < \theta < 90°)$$

$$\sin \theta = \frac{b}{c}$$

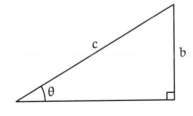

Tetra writes this in her notebook, whispering "Wow...wow..." as she does.

1.6 HOW TO REMEMBER SINE

Tetra   "I *must* have read this in my book, right?"

Me   "I'd think so. I can't imagine teaching trig functions without mentioning ratios of triangle side lengths."

Tetra   "I must have gotten lost in all the symbols."

Me   "Yeah? It doesn't seem like there's that many..."

Tetra   "It's not so much that there's a whole lot of them. The problem is that there's three sides, and I can never remember which ones go in the numerator and the denominator."

Me   "Oh, well here's a good trick for that. Using this triangle, write a cursive, lower-case 's' and say 'c divides b.' The 's' stands for 'sine,' and the 'c divides b' means you want the fraction $\frac{b}{c}$. Like this."[1]

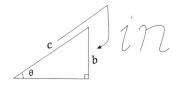

How to remember sin θ

---

[1]This is a mnemonic device commonly used in Japan. Readers unfamiliar with cursive script may have better success using mnemonics devised from the abbreviations SOH (sine = opposite ÷ hypotenuse), CAH (cosine = adjacent ÷ hypotenuse), and TOA (tangent = opposite ÷ adjacent), either simply as syllables (SOH-CAH-TOA) or by expanding those letters into a sentence, such as "Socks On Hard Concrete Always Hurts—Try Other Alternatives."

Tetra   "How do I remember where the right angle should be?"

Me   "Not a problem—you don't have to worry about where
            the right angle is, just where the angle you're taking
            the sine of is. You can just mentally move the triangle
            around so that θ is on the left."

Tetra   "Oh, okay."

Me   "Anyway, regardless of how you remember it, the most
            important thing is understanding what it is the sine func-
            tion is using, and what it's finding."

Tetra   "Maybe I don't quite understand that yet."

Me   "Sure you do. Like we said, once θ is set, that determines
            $\frac{b}{c}$. In other words, sine is a function that finds $\frac{b}{c}$ from
            $\angle\theta$."

            Tetra's eyes glimmer, as if she's come to a remark-
            able realization.

1.7 THE COSINE FUNCTION

Me   "Once you've come to grips with the sine function, the
            cosine function is a piece of cake. The only difference is
            that with the cosine function we're interested in sides a
            and c."

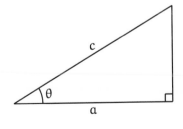

Me   "We're going to stretch side c without letting $\angle\theta$ change, just like before. For example, let's double the length of side c. Then here's what happens to the triangle."

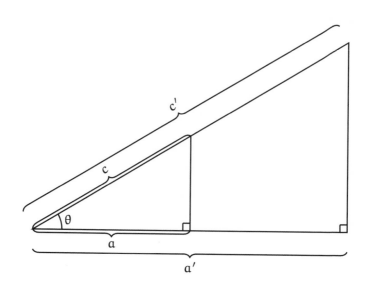

Tetra   "I guess side a doubled in length, too, to a'?"

Me   "Right. And this time we're saying that if the measure of $\angle\theta$ is kept constant, then the ratio of sides a and c will remain constant. The function $\cos\theta$ tells us the value of the fraction $\frac{a}{c}$ when we specify a value for θ."

Tetra   "So except for that one letter, it's just like $\sin\theta$!"

Definition of $\cos\theta$ as a ratio of two sides in a right triangle
$$(0° < \theta < 90°)$$

$$\cos\theta = \frac{a}{c}$$

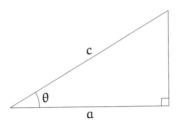

Me   "There's even a similar trick to remember it, using the 'c' for 'cosine.' This time, just say 'c divides a.' "

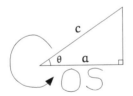

How to remember $\cos\theta$

Tetra   "Without forgetting to put $\angle\theta$ on the left!"

Me   "Good catch. And that's pretty much the basics of sine and cosine."

Tetra   "Cool! I understand everything so far!"

1.8 Removing Conditions

Me	"The next thing we want to do is get out from under this constraint that $0° < \theta < 90°$."

Tetra   "Why's that?"

Me   "Because it puts limits on what $\angle\theta$ can be, which makes it harder to deal with."

Tetra   "The fewer conditions the better, I guess. I always forget those."

Me   "You see where the condition comes from, right? Based on how we defined the sine function?"

Tetra   "I do! It's because if θ became $90°$ or larger, we wouldn't have a right triangle any more!"

Me   "That's right. That also means that we can't use triangles to define the sine function any more."

Tetra   "Well then what can we do?"

Me   "Use circles instead."

Tetra   "But how? Circles don't have angles, so... are there two kinds of sine?"

Me   "Two kinds?"

Tetra   "Like, one for triangles and one for circles."

Me   "No, no. They're all the same. We're going to work things so that when θ is in the range $0° < \theta < 90°$ nothing at all changes."

Tetra   "That sounds... hard."

Me   "Not really. We just need to make some minor adjustments."

Tetra   "If you say so..."

Me   "Some quick review first. Up until now, we've been defin-
              ing the sine function as the ratio of the lengths of two
              sides of a triangle. A fraction, in other words."

Definition of $\sin \theta$ as a ratio of two sides in a right triangle
$$(0° < \theta < 90°)$$

$$\sin \theta = \frac{b}{c}$$

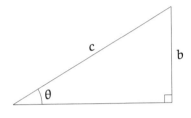

Tetra   "That looks right."

Me   "The important thing here is the value of that fraction $\frac{b}{c}$,
              so let's make things easy and think of the length of side c
              as being exactly 1."

Tetra   "Why do we want to do that?"

Me   "Because if $c = 1$, then $\sin \theta = \frac{b}{c} = \frac{b}{1} = b$. So nice and
              simple."

Tetra   "Uh, okay . . ."

Me   "This also means that since $\sin \theta = b$, the value of the
              sine function equals one of the side lengths."

Definition of $\sin\theta$ as a ratio of two sides in a right triangle
$(0° < \theta < 90°)$

$$\sin\theta = b \qquad \text{(when } c = 1\text{)}$$

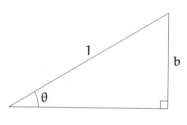

Me   "Let's put our right triangle on a coordinate plane, with the vertex of $\angle\theta$ on the origin and the right angle on the x-axis. Then let's name the point that isn't on an axis P."

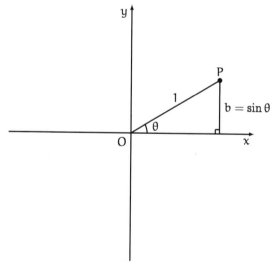

Placing the right triangle on a coordinate plane

Me "We've decided that c = 1, so the 'height' of point P equals sin θ."

Tetra "The height?"

Me "The distance above the x-axis."

Tetra "Ah, okay."

Me "So here's a question. If we keep increasing ∠θ, what kind of shape will point P trace out?"

A question

As we vary ∠θ, what shape does point P describe?

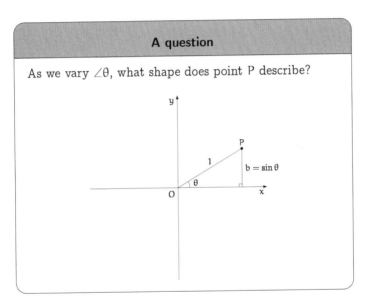

Tetra "I guess it will swing around... in a circle?"

Me "Right! The distance between point O and point P will still be 1, so point P will move in a circle. Just like drawing one with a compass."

Tetra "Ooh, that's fun!"

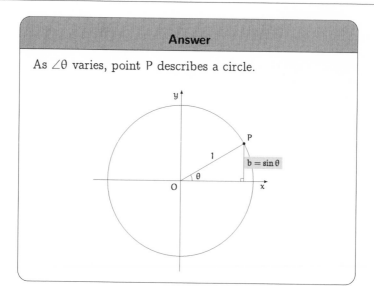

Answer

As $\angle\theta$ varies, point P describes a circle.

Me "A circle with a radius of 1 is called a unit circle. We've centered this one on the origin."

Tetra holds up a hand to stop me and writes in her notebook.

Tetra "Unit circle... Okay, I'm good. But why are we making circles?"

Me "Because they let us escape from the confines of the right triangle."

Tetra "The right triangle was confining us?"

Me "Sure, so long as we were relying on it to define $\sin\theta$. For example, it would be nice if the sine function had a value when $\theta = 0°$, but we can't make a triangle in that case."

Tetra "Ah, because that would flatten the triangle out into a line."

Me "That's right. But if we define $\sin\theta$ using a circle, we can say its value is just the y-value of this point P."

Tetra   "Where did that come from?"

Me   "Just look at the graph. You'll see."

Defining $\sin\theta$ as the y-coordinate of a point P on the unit circle.

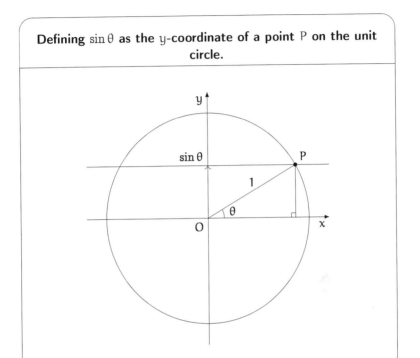

Tetra   "Hmm..."

Me   "Do you see how when we define it like this, nothing's changed from when we used the triangle for angles $0° < \theta < 90°$?"

Tetra   "Sure! I can still see the triangle and everything. And now I totally get what you mean by the height of that point."

Me   "Maybe I shouldn't have used that word, though, since sometimes that 'height' will be negative."

Tetra   "Negative height?"

Me   "It can be. Like when θ looks like this."

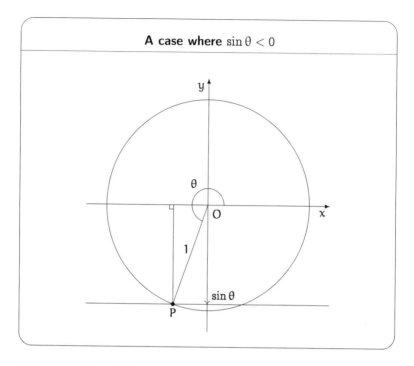

A case where $\sin \theta < 0$

Tetra   "I see! That happens when the point dips down below the x-axis."

Me   "It's easy to see what's going on if you watch θ gradually increase, like this."

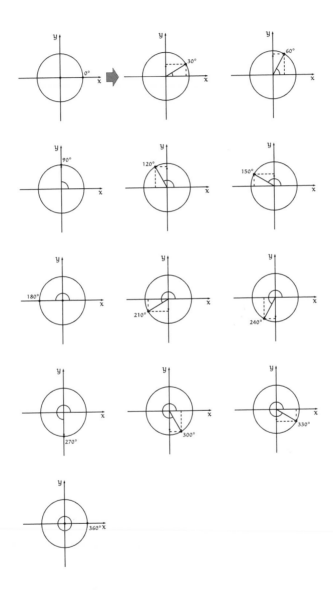

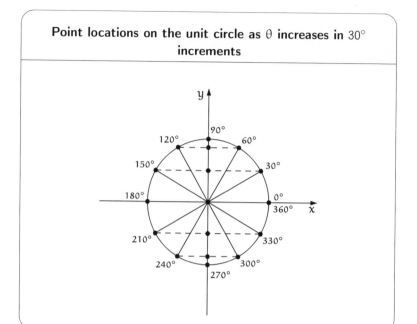

Point locations on the unit circle as θ increases in 30° increments

Tetra   "Ooh! Ooh! I think I found something! Is this true?"

$$-1 \leqslant \sin \theta \leqslant 1$$

Me   "Nice! How'd you get that?"

Tetra   "Well, since the point stays on a circle whose radius is 1, the y-coordinate will be 1 when it's on the top, and −1 when it's on the bottom. You said that $\sin \theta$ equals the value of the y-coordinate, so that should mean it can never get bigger than 1, or smaller than −1."

Me   "A wonderful discovery, and you're absolutely right— $-1 \leqslant \sin \theta \leqslant 1$ will be true for any value of θ. That's a property that comes straight out of its definition."

1.9 SINE CURVES

Miruka   "You guys seem to be having fun."

Tetra   "Hi, Miruka! Look! I'm learning trigonometry!"

Miruka often joined Tetra and me in our after-hours math talks. She cocks her head and peeks at what we'd been writing.

Miruka   "Hmph. No sine curves yet."

Tetra   "What's a sine curve?"

Miruka sits next to Tetra and snatches the pencil from my hand. She acts as cool as ever, but I can see through that—she's just itching to take the teacher's seat.

Miruka   "What are the horizontal and vertical axes you're using in this coordinate plane?"

Tetra   "Um...the x-axis and the y-axis?"

Miruka   "Good. So for a point (x, y) on the unit circle, the circle represents the relationship between x and y."

Me   "It's a restriction on what they can be."

Tetra   "Sure, just like when we were using quadratic functions to draw parabolas."[2]

Miruka   "Let's make a new graph, one where the horizontal axis is a θ-axis instead of an x-axis. We'll keep the y-axis as it is."

Tetra   "A θ-axis?"

Me   "You'll see what she means."

Miruka smiles and nods. I see that math-mode twinkle in her eye.

Miruka   "Say that the angle is $0°$. Then we plot points on each graph like this."

---

[2]See Chapter 5 of *Math Girls Talk About Equations and Graphs*

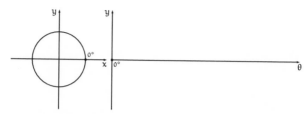

Plotting points on each graph when $\theta = 0°$

Tetra   "Lemme see if I've got this straight. The graph on the right has a horizontal θ-axis, so the coordinates there are (θ, y). That means when $\theta = 0°$ we say $y = \sin 0°$, which is 0. So there's a point at $(0, 0)$. Is that right?"

Miruka   "Perfect. Now let's do it with $\theta = 30°$. When we make θ bigger, the point is going to move in different ways on the two graphs. On the left graph, the point will spin around in a circle. On the right, it will keep advancing."

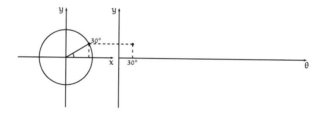

Tetra   "It advances...Oh, I see that. But the height of the point will be the same on both graphs, right?"

Me   "Sure, because they're both using the same y-axis."

Miruka   "On to $\theta = 60°$. On the left we've spun twice as far along the circle, while on the right we've moved ahead twice as far."

Tetra   "Ah, okay, this thing about a θ-axis is starting to make more sense."

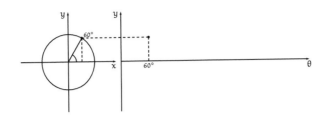

Miruka   "Add another 30°, so θ = 90° now."

Tetra   "And sin 90° = 1! We've reached the top of the circle!"

Me   "Or the maximum value of sin θ, if you want to look at
           it that way."

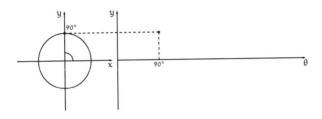

Miruka   "Another 30°, to θ = 120°."

Tetra   "What goes up, must come down."

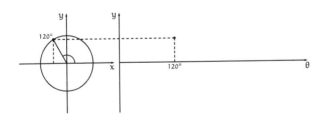

Miruka   "And another 30° ..."

Tetra   "Up to θ = 150° now."

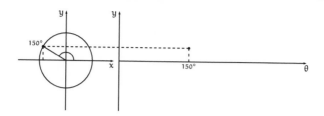

Miruka   "And now at $\theta = 180°$ ..."

Tetra   "Boom, we hit the floor. So $\sin 180° = 0$."

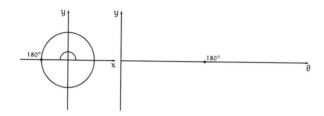

Me   "We're going to crash right through that floor, though."

Tetra   "Oh, right! Now's when we dip under the x-axis and go negative. I guess we're up to $\theta = 210°$ next?"

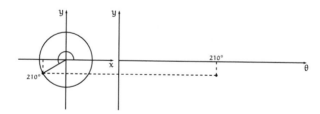

Miruka   "And then on to $240°$."

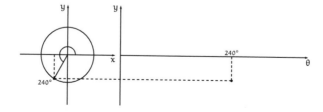

Tetra   "Wow, I don't think I've ever used an angle like 240°
           before."

Miruka   "Because of symmetry."

Tetra   "Symmetry?"

Miruka   "Later. Let's move ahead to 270°."

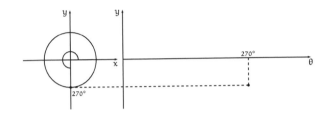

Tetra   "And we've hit rock bottom. So $\sin 270° = -1$!"

Me   "The minimum value for $\sin \theta$."

Tetra   "So $\sin \theta$ is biggest when $\theta = 90°$, and smallest when
           $\theta = 270°$. Hang on, I gotta write this down..."

Miruka   "While you're doing that, I'm moving on to 300°."

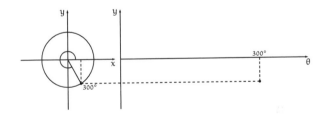

Miruka   "And to 330°."

Tetra   "We're repeating ourselves, aren't we? We pass through
           the same heights as we go up and then back down, and
           then do the same thing with negative heights when we're
           under the axis."

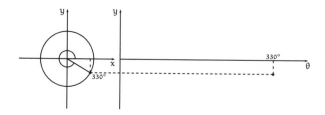

Miruka   "We end up back at home with 360°."

Tetra   "All the way around and back where we started. So
            $\sin 360° = 0$."

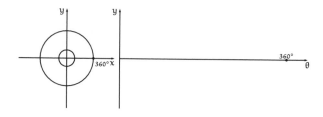

Me   "The big question is, do you see the sine curve?"

Tetra   "I do! It comes from the up-down-up on the left making
            waves on the right!"

Miruka   "And that wave is the sine curve. If we draw the curve
            instead of just plotting points, here's what we get."

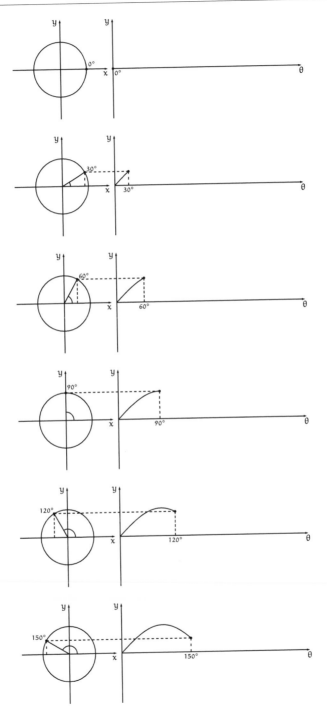

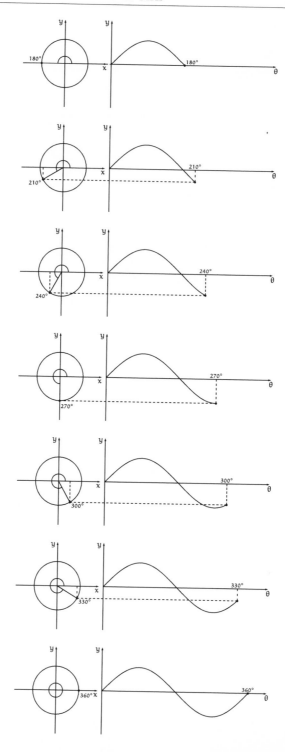

Tetra   "It's so...pretty!"

Me   "I agree. It is pretty."

Miruka   "It's *beautiful*. Such an elegant correspondence between
            the unit circle and the sine curve."

Correspondence between the unit circle and the sine curve

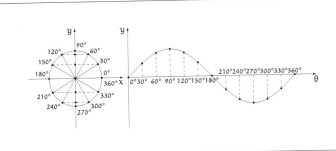

Tetra   "So what does the cosine curve look like?"

Miruka   "The cosine curve?"

Tetra   "Well, we just graphed $\sin\theta$ to get the sine curve, right?
            Seems like we should be able to graph $\cos\theta$ and get a
            cosine curve, too."

Miruka   "You can graph $\cos\theta$, but you don't call that a cosine
            curve. It gives you another sine curve."

Tetra   "Huh? Why?"

Miruka   "The graphs of $\sin\theta$ and $\cos\theta$ are similar, with just one
            minor difference. I'm pretty sure you could graph it
            yourself if you tried."

Tetra   "You sure about that?"

Miruka   "When you defined $\sin\theta$ using a circle, the value of $\sin\theta$
            was just the y-coordinate of a point on the circle, right?
            Well $\cos\theta$ is the x-coordinate. Knowing that should be
            enough to graph the cosine function."

Defining $\cos\theta$ as the x-coordinate of a point P on the unit circle.

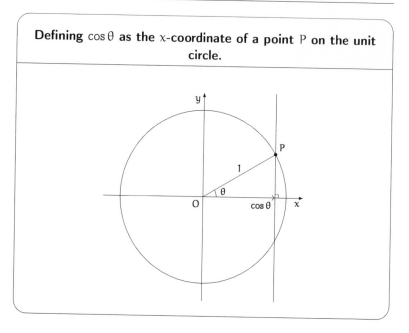

Ms. Mizutani "The library is *closed!*"

With her announcement that it was time to go home, Ms. Mizutani shut down yet another math talk. As I walked home, I wondered if Tetra would be successful in graphing the cosine function...

"If name is sufficient to represent form, then a name is all you need."

APPENDIX: GREEK LETTERS

Lowercase	Uppercase	Name
α	A	alpha
β	B	beta
γ	Γ	gamma
δ	Δ	delta
ε ε	E	epsilon
ζ	Z	zeta
η	H	eta
θ ϑ	Θ	theta
ι	I	iota
κ ϰ	K	kappa
λ	Λ	lambda
μ	M	mu
ν	N	nu
ξ	Ξ	xi
o	O	omicron
π ϖ	Π	pi
ρ	P	rho
σ	Σ	sigma
τ	T	tau
υ	Υ	upsilon
φ φ	Φ	phi
χ	X	chi
ψ	Ψ	psi
ω	Ω	omega

APPENDIX: VALUES OF TRIGONOMETRIC FUNCTIONS FOR
COMMON ANGLES

The angles $30°$, $45°$, and $60°$ are frequently used in a variety of
problems. Let's find the values of the sine and cosine functions for
those angles.

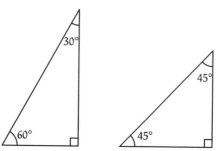

Right triangles with $30°$, $45°$, and $60°$ angles

We'll start with the $30°$ and $60°$ angles. If you place two right
triangles having a $60°$ angle back-to-back, you get a triangle $\triangle ABB'$
with three $60°$ angles, as in the diagram below. Since each angle has
the same measure $\triangle ABB'$ is an equilateral triangle, so we know that
$\overline{BB'} = \overline{AB}$.

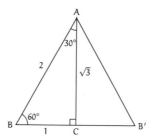

Letting $\overline{BC} = 1$, we have that $\overline{B'C} = 1$ and $\overline{BB'} = \overline{AB} = 2$.
Let's apply the Pythagorean theorem to the right triangle $\triangle ABC$ to

find $\overline{AC}$.

$$\overline{BC}^2 + \overline{AC}^2 = \overline{AB}^2 \qquad \text{the Pythagorean theorem}$$
$$1^2 + \overline{AC}^2 = 2^2 \qquad \text{because } \overline{BC} = 1 \text{ and } \overline{AB} = 2$$
$$\overline{AC}^2 = 3$$
$$\overline{AC} = \sqrt{3}$$

From this we find that $\overline{AC} = \sqrt{3}$. Now we can find the other values:

$$\cos 30° = \frac{\overline{AC}}{\overline{AB}} = \frac{\sqrt{3}}{2}$$
$$\cos 60° = \frac{\overline{BC}}{\overline{AB}} = \frac{1}{2}$$
$$\sin 30° = \frac{\overline{BC}}{\overline{AB}} = \frac{1}{2}$$
$$\sin 60° = \frac{\overline{AC}}{\overline{AB}} = \frac{\sqrt{3}}{2}$$

Now let's look at 45° angles. In $\triangle DEF$, the measure of both $\angle D$ and $\angle E$ is 45°, so $\triangle DEF$ is an isosceles triangle with $\overline{DF} = \overline{EF}$.

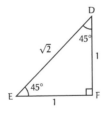

Letting $\overline{DF} = \overline{EF} = 1$, we can use the Pythagorean theorem again to find $\overline{DE}$:

$$\overline{DF}^2 + \overline{EF}^2 = \overline{DE}^2 \qquad \text{the Pythagorean theorem}$$
$$1^2 + 1^2 = \overline{DE}^2 \qquad \text{because } \overline{DF} = \overline{EF} = 1$$
$$\overline{DE}^2 = 2$$
$$\overline{DE} = \sqrt{2}$$

So we've found that $\overline{DE} = \sqrt{2}$. From this, we can find the following values:

$$\cos 45° = \frac{\overline{EF}}{\overline{DE}} = \frac{1}{\sqrt{2}} = \frac{\sqrt{2}}{2}$$

$$\sin 45° = \frac{\overline{DF}}{\overline{DE}} = \frac{1}{\sqrt{2}} = \frac{\sqrt{2}}{2}$$

These results are summarized below:

Values of trigonometric functions for some common angles

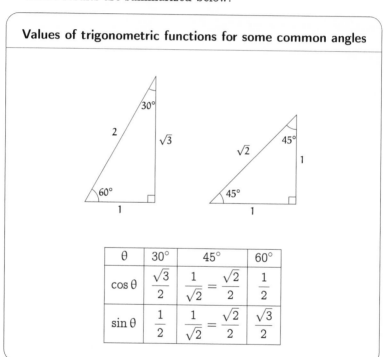

θ	$30°$	$45°$		$60°$
$\cos \theta$	$\dfrac{\sqrt{3}}{2}$	$\dfrac{1}{\sqrt{2}}$	$= \dfrac{\sqrt{2}}{2}$	$\dfrac{1}{2}$
$\sin \theta$	$\dfrac{1}{2}$	$\dfrac{1}{\sqrt{2}}$	$= \dfrac{\sqrt{2}}{2}$	$\dfrac{\sqrt{3}}{2}$

Problems for Chapter 1

"First, we have to *understand* the problem; we have to see clearly what is required."

GEORGE PÓLYA
How To Solve It, 2nd Ed.

Problem 1-1 (Finding $\sin\theta$)

Find the value of $\sin 45°$, without looking at the appendix to this chapter.

(Answer on page 227)

Problem 1-2 (Finding θ from $\sin\theta$)

Find all possible values for θ in the range $0° \leqslant \theta \leqslant 360°$ for which $\sin\theta = \frac{1}{2}$.

(Answer on page 228)

Problem 1-3 (Finding $\cos\theta$)

Find the value of $\cos 0°$.

(Answer on page 230)

Problem 1-4 (Finding θ from $\cos\theta$)

Find all possible values for θ in the range $0° \leqslant \theta \leqslant 360°$ for which $\cos\theta = \frac{1}{2}$.

(Answer on page 230)

Problem 1-5 (Graphing $x = \cos\theta$)

Draw a graph of $x = \cos\theta$ for values of θ in the range $0° \leqslant \theta \leqslant 360°$. In the graph, use values of θ for the horizontal axis, and values of x for the vertical axis.

(Answer on page 232)

CHAPTER 2

Back and Forth

"There's nothing unusual about going
and returning..."

2.1 IN MY ROOM

Yuri   "Hey, cuz. What's this?"

My cousin Yuri lived up the street, and often came over to hang out.
She was holding a piece of paper I'd left lying about.

Me   "Some graphs we made the other day."

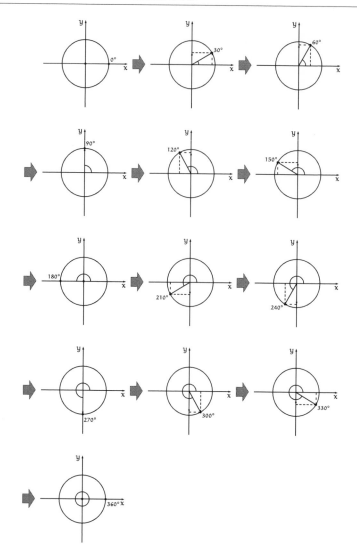

Yuri   "This looks like fun. What's it all about?"

Yuri's ponytail bobs as she moves her head back
and forth, following the graphs in order.

Me   "It's loads of fun. You start with a unit circle, centered
on the origin—"

Yuri   "What's a unit circle?"

Me   "A circle with a radius of 1."

Yuri   "Oh."

Me   "Then you move a point on the circle in 30° increments."

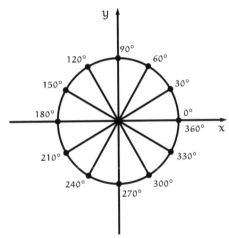

A point traveling along the unit circle in 30° increments

Yuri   "So it's making a loop."

Me   "A circle, right. So 360° and 0° put you at the same place."

Yuri   "And what's the point of all this?"

Me   "That you can use the unit circle to define the trigonometric functions."

Yuri   "Right over my head."

Me   "It's not so bad. You just find the x-coordinate of the point and call it the 'cosine,' and the y-coordinate is called the 'sine.'"

Yuri   "Oh, the sine and cosine! I've heard of those!"

Me   "Well there you go. Call the angle of rotation 'theta,'
            and you're done."

- The x-coordinate is $\cos\theta$.

- The y-coordinate is $\sin\theta$.

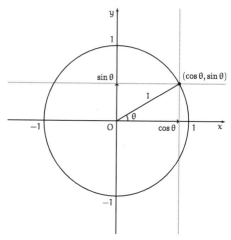

A point (x, y) on the unit circle equals $(\cos\theta, \sin\theta)$

Yuri   "Why like that?"

Me   "No real reason, that's just how $\cos\theta$ and $\sin\theta$ are de-
            fined. They get used a lot, so they need a name."

Yuri   "What, like 'Ms. Cosine' and 'Mr. Sine'?"

Me   "I guess. The word 'trigonometry' makes everything
            sound harder than it is. Draw a unit circle, put a point
            on it, change θ to make the point move, find its
            x and y values, and that's pretty much all there is to it.
            That's the basics at least. Even so, you can do lots of
            cool stuff using just sine and cosine."

Yuri   "Cool for a certain kind of person, I guess. So what's with all the lines on this one?"

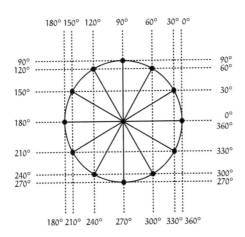

Me   "That's just me messing around, connecting some points."

Yuri   "What are these numbers?"

Me   "Angles. I was just looking at how points connect with other points for certain values of θ."

Yuri   "Huh."

Me   "Cosine is the x-coordinate, so when the angle changes the cosine value moves back and forth on the horizontal axis. Sine is the y-coordinate, so its value moves up and down on the vertical axis. "

Yuri   "Yeah?"

Me   "See it? The vertical lines are the cosines, and the horizontal lines are the sines."

Yuri   "You should have labeled these like $\cos 0°$ and $\sin 30°$, not just $0°$ and $30°$."

Me   "If I was going to use the graph for anything important.
          But I was just doodling."

Yuri   "Looks kinda like a clock, doesn't it."

Me   "I guess. I split it up into 30° increments, so there's even
          12 sections. There's those lines coming out of the center,
          too. The angle usually increases in the counter-clockwise
          direction, though."

Yuri   "I think it looks like a clock even without the lines."

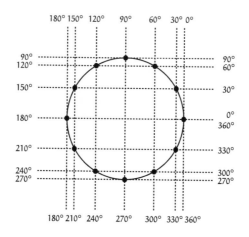

Me   "I suppose it does."

Yuri   "Kinda cool how you're making intersections on a circle,
          but what you get looks like intersections on a city map."

Me   "Huh. I never looked at it that way, but you're right."

Yuri   "Kind of a weird city, though, to have blocks that get
          bigger and smaller like that . . . "

          Yuri narrows her eyes and leans in for a closer
          look at the graph.

Yuri   "There's seven lines in each direction, right?"

Me   "The horizontal and vertical lines, you mean?   Yeah,
            there are."

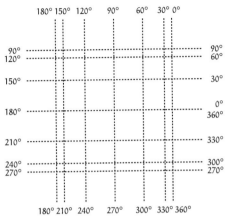

There are seven horizontal and seven vertical lines

Yuri   "So that means there's 49 intersections, right?   7 × 7?"

Me   "Sure."

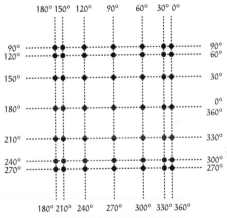

The 49 intersections

Yuri   "That's a whole lotta intersections.   Seems you should
            be able to make way more interesting shapes than just
            a boring old circle."

Me	"Yuri, that's an *excellent* idea!"
Yuri	"Whoa, what's got you so excited all of a sudden?"
Me	"I just remembered something cool! C'mon, let's draw some graphs!"
Yuri	"Uh oh. What have I started..."

2.2 DRAWING GRAPHS

Me	"Remember how I said the x-coordinate of a point on a unit circle gives you $\cos\theta$, and the y-coordinate gives you $\sin\theta$?"
Yuri	"Yeah?"
Me	"Well both of those use the same angle."
Yuri	"I'd think so. And?"
Me	"Look at it the other way—when we feed the same theta to both the sine and the cosine function, we get a unit circle. In other words, points $(x,y) = (\cos\theta, \sin\theta)$ describe a unit circle."
Yuri	"Sure."
Me	"So what would happen if we give them *different* angles? Say we separate the angles we feed to the cosine and the sine by 30°? Like, we plot $(x,y) = (\cos\theta, \sin(\theta + 30°))$, instead? I wonder what shape we would get."
Yuri	"You've completely lost me."
Me	"Nah, you'll get it. Let me show you using a graph. Like, if we plot a point using 0° for both the horizontal and vertical directions, it goes here, right?"

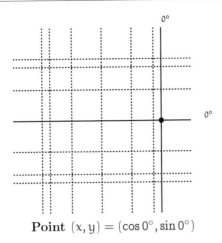

Point $(x, y) = (\cos 0°, \sin 0°)$

Yuri   "Yeah, okay."

Me   "And if we start from this point $(\cos 0°, \sin 0°)$ and work our way around, we get a unit circle, right?"

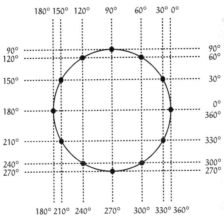

The figure described by $(x, y) = (\cos \theta, \sin \theta)$

Yuri   "That's what you said, so I suppose we do."

Me   "Well let's see what happens when the sine function leads by 30°. That means the horizontal lines will be leading by one step. For example, we start here, at point $(\cos 0°, \sin 30°)$."

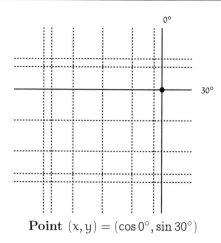

Point $(x, y) = (\cos 0°, \sin 30°)$

Yuri   "Okay, I see where you're going with this. Go on."

Me   "So the problem is this: if you spin theta all the way from
            0 degrees back to 360, with the horizontal line always 30°
            ahead of the vertical line, what kind of shape do we get?"

Problem

The point $(x, y) = (\cos \theta, \sin \theta)$ describes a unit circle.

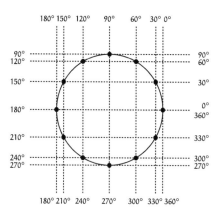

What shape does $(x, y) = (\cos \theta, \sin(\theta + 30°))$ describe?

Yuri   "Hmm..."

Me   "Let's give it a shot. The next step will be the 30° ver-
          tical line, and the 60° horizontal one. In other words,
          point $(\cos 30°, \sin 60°)$."

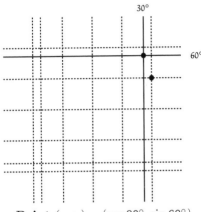

Point $(x, y) = (\cos 30°, \sin 60°)$

Yuri   "Huh, it went way up. Maybe we're going to get a bigger
          circle?"

Me   "Let's see. In the next step, the x-coordinate will be
          $\cos 60°$. So what will the sine be?"

Yuri   "I guess 90° comes after 60°?"

Me   "Right. So the y-coordinate is $\sin 90°$, which is here. Oh,
          this is going to be so cool..."

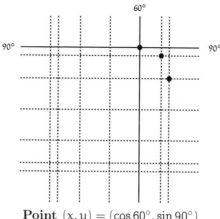

Point $(x, y) = (\cos 60°, \sin 90°)$

Yuri   "See? I think we *are* getting a big circle."

Me   "We'll see. Let's plot $(\cos 90°, \sin 120°)$."

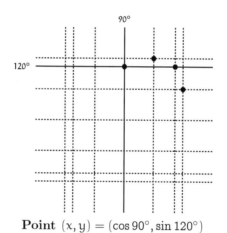

Point $(x, y) = (\cos 90°, \sin 120°)$

Yuri   "Well, so much for the big circle theory."

Me   "The next step is $(\cos 120°, \sin 150°)$."

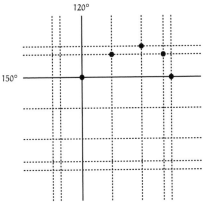

Point $(x, y) = (\cos 120°, \sin 150°)$

Yuri "Oh, I get it! It isn't a circle, it's an oval!"

Me "Starting to look that way. On to $(\cos 150°, \sin 180°)$."

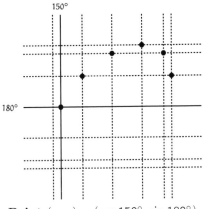

Point $(x, y) = (\cos 150°, \sin 180°)$

Yuri "Hey, let me plot some. We don't even have to think about the functions any more, just advance line-by-line."

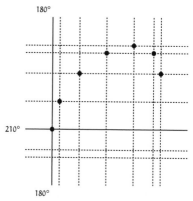

Point $(x, y) = (\cos 180°, \sin 210°)$

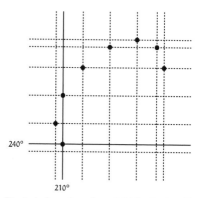

Point $(x, y) = (\cos 210°, \sin 240°)$

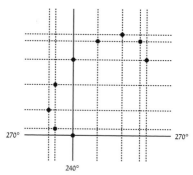

Point $(x, y) = (\cos 240°, \sin 270°)$

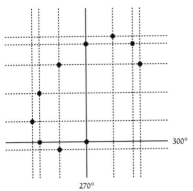

Point $(x, y) = (\cos 270°, \sin 300°)$

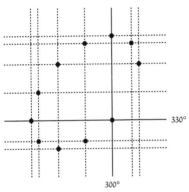

Point $(x, y) = (\cos 300°, \sin 330°)$

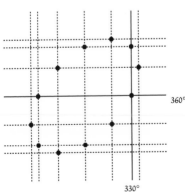

Point $(x, y) = (\cos 330°, \sin 360°)$

Yuri   "And...done!"

Me   "Looks like you were right. A 30° lead makes an oval."

Yuri   "Neat!"

Answer

Point $(x, y) = (\cos \theta, \sin \theta)$ describes a circle.

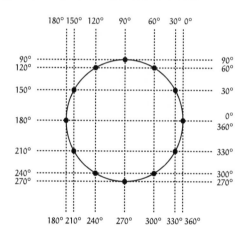

Point $(x, y) = (\cos \theta, \sin(\theta + 30°))$ describes an oval.

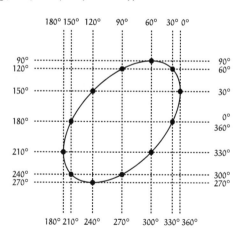

2.3 FURTHER AHEAD

Me   "So I wonder what happens if we move the sine function
          ahead by 60°, instead of 30°?"

Yuri   "I got this one!"

          Yuri's pencil is in constant motion as she draws
          the graph.

Me   "Done?"

Yuri   "Yep! Another oval, but a skinnier one!"

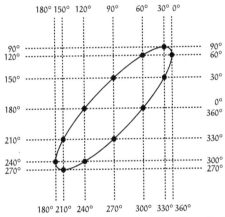

The figure described by point $(x, y) = (\cos\theta, \sin(\theta + 60°))$

Me   "Well then how about—"

Yuri   "—oh, 90°!"

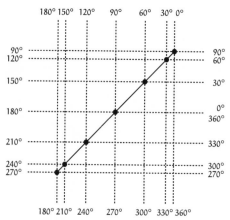

The figure described by point $(x, y) = (\cos\theta, \sin(\theta + 90°))$

Me   "Flat as a pancake."

Yuri   "Yeah, it just goes back and forth, through the same points."

2.4 SLOWING THINGS DOWN

Yuri   "This is way cool."

Me   "Let's see what happens if we go the other way, and delay the horizontal lines by 30°."

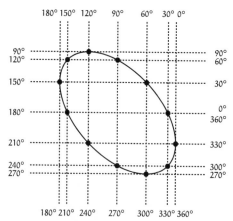

The figure described by point $(x, y) = (\cos\theta, \sin(\theta - 30°))$

Yuri   "And by 60°!"

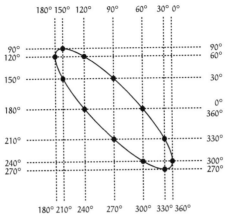

The figure described by point $(x, y) = (\cos\theta, \sin(\theta - 60°))$

Me   "Delaying by 90° flattens it out again."

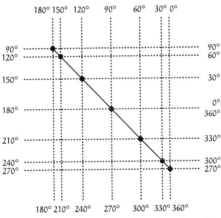

The figure described by point $(x, y) = (\cos\theta, \sin(\theta - 90°))$

Yuri   "So if you shift the angles like that, it's ovals all over the place."

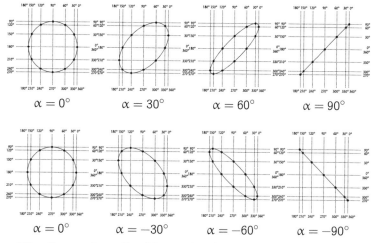

The figure described by point $(x, y) = (\cos\theta, \sin(\theta + \alpha))$

Me "It looks like a circle seen from different angles. I guess the line one is the circle seen from the side. Kinda interesting how all of these are made from the 49 intersections you noticed."

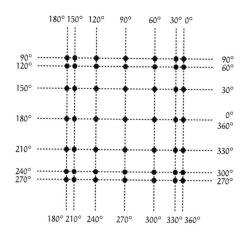

Yuri "Who'da thunk it!"

Me "Let's try something new!"

2.5 DOUBLING DOWN

Yuri   "So what's next?"

Me   "Hmm...Last time we just shifted the angles by the
            same amount for each line. How about we try increas-
            ing the horizontal line by 60° each time the vertical line
            moves ahead 30°."

Yuri   "So you're doubling stuff? This time we've *gotta* get
            something bigger."

Me   "I don't think so, since we haven't changed the radius."

Yuri   "Good point. I guess we can't leave these 49 intersec-
            tions, no matter what we do. I can't picture what it's
            going to look like, though."

Me   "When we drew the ovals, the horizontal and vertical
            lines advanced by one each, right?"

Yuri   "Yeah?"

Me   "And when we got to an edge we, like, bounced back."

Yuri   "Sure."

Me   "Anyway, this time when we move the vertical line one
            jump left or right, we'll be moving the horizontal line by
            two up or down. So the question is, what kind of shape
            does that make?"

Yuri   "I can't wait to find out!"

Me   "Well then let's get to graphing. First—"

Yuri   "Whoa! Hold up! I want to try to think this one out."

Me   "Be my guest."

Yuri enters deep think mode, twiddling her ponytail. It was like
pulling teeth to get her to work on a problem she didn't like, but
when she latched on to one that interested her, there was no holding
her back.

Yuri   "Nope. I'm not seeing it."

Me   "Let's try graphing it, then."

Yuri   "Sure. I did notice one thing, though."

Me   "What's that?"

Yuri   "Every time we move the vertical line by 30°, we move
            the horizontal one by 60°, right?"

Me   "Right."

Yuri   "Doesn't that mean that every time the vertical line has
            looped around, the horizontal one has looped twice?"

Me   "Huh, I guess it does, yeah."

Yuri   "Hmm, maybe it's weird to call it looping. It's the point
            that's revolving around a circle. The lines are like, what,
            going back and forth?"

Me   "Right. So each time the vertical line makes a round trip,
            the horizontal line has made two."

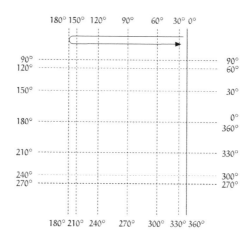

By the time the vertical line has made a round trip...

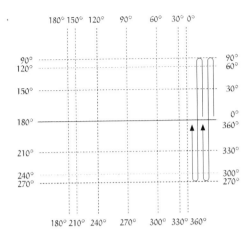

...the horizontal one has made two.

Yuri   "A round trip, right. That's the phrase I was looking for."

Me   "So let's graph it and see what happens."

Yuri   "Cool!"

Me   "Like usual, we'll start from the 0° angle on the unit circle. That would be where the horizontal and vertical lines are both 0°."

Yuri   "Right."

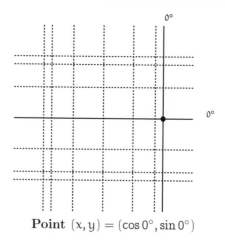

Point $(x, y) = (\cos 0°, \sin 0°)$

Me   "Okay, next step. We want the vertical line to go one step to the left, and the horizontal line two steps up. So the angle on the vertical line is 30°, and on the horizontal line it's 60°."

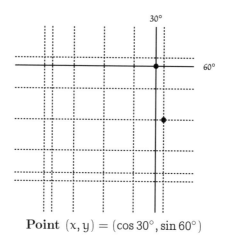

Point $(x, y) = (\cos 30°, \sin 60°)$

Yuri   "That one I could see—a big jump up and over. After that it gets tricky."

Me   "Yeah, it does. We want to move the vertical line left by one and the horizontal up by two, but we've got to be careful. We want to move 60° from 60°, so we need to end up at 120°. So by going up two, we've bounced off the top and ended up back down where we started."

Yuri   "Ah, okay. *That's* what you meant by the line bouncing."

Me   "Yeah, it looks like we haven't moved at all, but really we've just made a U-turn."

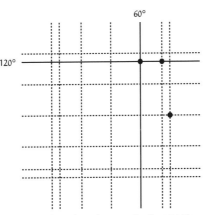

Point $(x, y) = (\cos 60°, \sin 120°)$

Yuri   "Okay, I'm good with that. Still hard to see what this shape is going to be, though."

Me   "Let's keep going then. So we move the vertical line by 30° again, to 90° this time. And the horizontal line moves by 60°, to 180°."

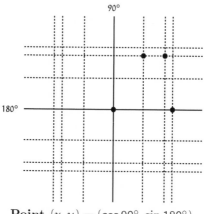

Point $(x, y) = (\cos 90°, \sin 180°)$

Yuri   "Maybe we're getting another oval after all. Another long skinny one."

Me   "Hmm, maybe."

Yuri   "You don't sound convinced."

Me   "We need more points first. Next is 120° for the vertical, 240° for the horizontal."

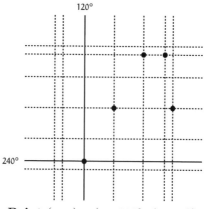

Point $(x, y) = (\cos 120°, \sin 240°)$

Yuri   "If this is an oval, it's about to spill over!"

Me   "I think it's time to give up on the oval. If you think about symmetry, you can probably guess what's going to happen."

Yuri   "What symmetry?"

Me   "You'll see. Our next point is at the intersection of 150° and 300°."

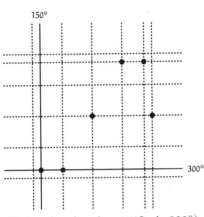

Point $(x, y) = (\cos 150°, \sin 300°)$

Yuri   "What's up with that? We're curving back!"

Me   "We are indeed."

Yuri   "But won't it, like, collide with itself?"

Me   "Nothing wrong with that. Onward, to the 180° and 360° point. Now the horizontal line has made one round trip, and the vertical line is halfway there."

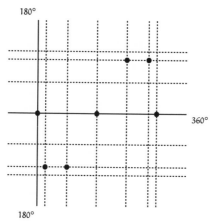

Point $(x, y) = (\cos 180°, \sin 360°)$

Yuri   "Not at all what I would have guessed. It's turning into, what, an S shape?"

Me   "A crooked one, so far. But it's still only half done. Do you see what the other half will look like?"

Yuri   "Um...I think so. Looks like we're going to flip the S over, so we'll get a figure eight."

Me   "Let's finish up and see. The vertical line is at 210°, and when we go 60° from 360°, we end up at 60°."

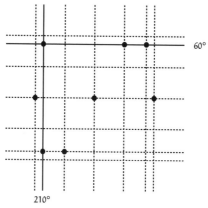

Point $(x, y) = (\cos 210°, \sin 60°)$

Yuri   "Okay, now I see the symmetry you were talking about. I guess we don't even really have to calculate anything from here on out."

Me   "That's right. It's pretty easy to see where the rest of the points go."

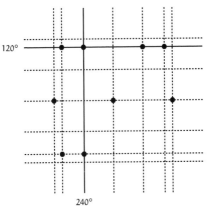

Point $(x, y) = (\cos 240°, \sin 120°)$

Yuri   "Next we land on a point we've already plotted."

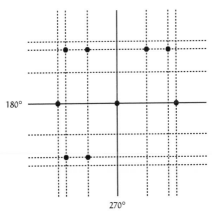

Point $(x, y) = (\cos 270°, \sin 180°)$

Me   "The collision you were worried about. But that's not a
            problem."

Yuri   "Next we go way down to the right."

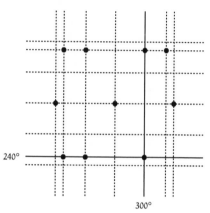

Point $(x, y) = (\cos 300°, \sin 240°)$

Me   "Yep."

Yuri   "Then finally we just scootch over to here."

Me   "Or bounce off the bottom, depending on how you look
            at it."

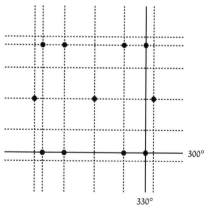

Point $(x, y) = (\cos 330°, \sin 300°)$

Yuri   "And done! That's a full trip around!"

Me   "Well, the vertical line would say it made a full trip around. The horizontal one might say it made two trips."

Yuri   "Looks like I was right! It *is* a figure eight!"

Me   "One on its side, I guess. Or an infinity symbol. Anyway, that's what we get when the horizontal line moves twice as fast as the vertical one. Interesting..."

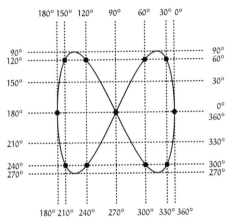

The figure described by $(x, y) = (\cos\theta, \sin 2\theta)$

2.6 More Graphs

Yuri   "Let's do some more!"

Me   "Seriously?"

Yuri   "This is cool! I want to see what else we can make."

Me   "I dunno. Sounds like too much work. I want to just, like, *bam* get an answer."

Yuri   "Nice try, but your impersonation of me is all kinds of lame."

Me   "Hey, I have an idea. How about if we do what we just
            did, with the horizontal line moving twice as fast as the
            vertical one, but starting 30° off. So we start from here."

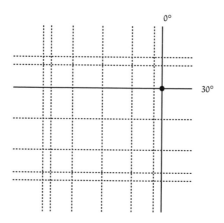

Yuri   "When we did that with a circle it turned into an oval.
            So I guess this will ovalize the figure eight shape?"

Me   "Nice prediction. Let's see."

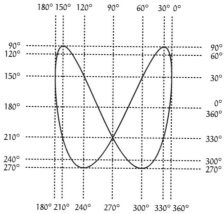

The figure described by point $(x, y) = (\cos\theta, \sin(2\theta + 30°))$

Yuri   "Hmm . . . Not really what I was imagining."

Me   "Yeah, calling those ovals is a bit of a stretch."

Yuri   "It's more like the figure eight is drooping or something."

Me   "Let's try starting from other places. Maybe there's a
          pattern."

Yuri   "There always is, isn't there."

Me   "Let's do one offset by 60°."

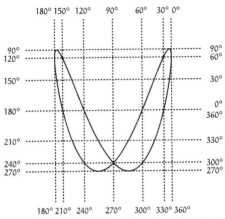

The figure described by point $(x, y) = (\cos\theta, \sin(2\theta + 60°))$

Yuri   "Huh."

Me   "I guess we should do 90°, too, for good measure."

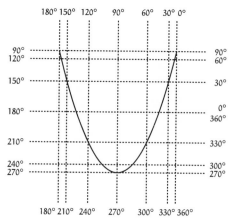

The figure described by point $(x, y) = (\cos\theta, \sin(2\theta + 90°))$

Yuri	"Now that's just weird."
Me	"Yeah, strange how things change just by varying where you start from."
Yuri	"Whoa, hang on. I think I'm starting to see the bigger picture here."
Me	"What do you mean?"
Yuri	"When we did the circle and ovals, remember how you said the ovals were like looking at a tilted circle? Well the first figure eight kinda looks like a circle twisted in half, and now we're tilting *that*."
Me	"A twisted circle, huh. I like it."
Yuri	"Let's make a few more."

Yuri and I spend the rest of the afternoon exploring these graphs.

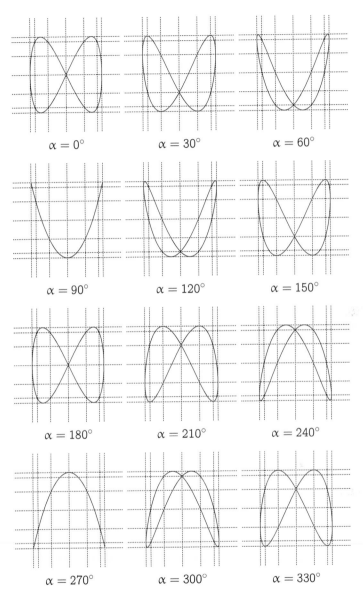

The figure described by point $(x, y) = (\cos\theta, \sin(2\theta + \alpha))$

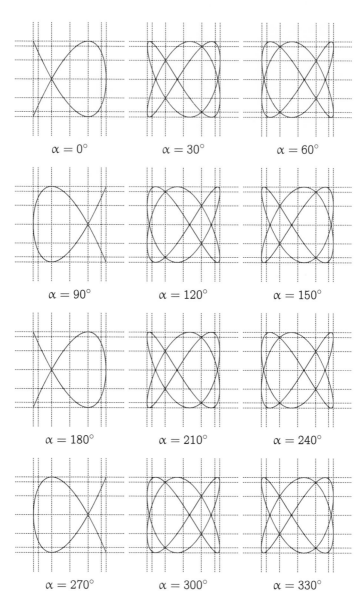

The figure described by point $(x, y) = (\cos 2\theta, \sin(3\theta + \alpha))$

Yuri	"Okay, that was fun, but I'm beat. So where'd you get the idea to do this, anyway?"
Me	"My physics teacher. They're called Lissajous curves, by the way."
Yuri	"Wow, they have a name and everything. Hang on, your *physics* teacher? Not math?"
Me	"Yeah. She showed us how to make them using a machine called an oscilloscope when we were doing an electronics experiment, and let us explore the math behind them for extra credit."
Yuri	"Wow, high school sounds like a lot more fun than middle school."
Me	"It is. Well, usually. Depends on the teacher, I guess."
Yuri	"Don't it always..."
Mom	"Anybody want pizza?"
Yuri	"Like you even have to ask! We're coming!"

Lured by my mother's summons, we headed for the dining room. After all, math is eternal; hot pizza isn't.

"...it's when we go together that the mystery begins."

APPENDIX: LISSAJOUS CURVE GRAPHING PAPER

Feel free to copy this page to create your own Lissajous curves.

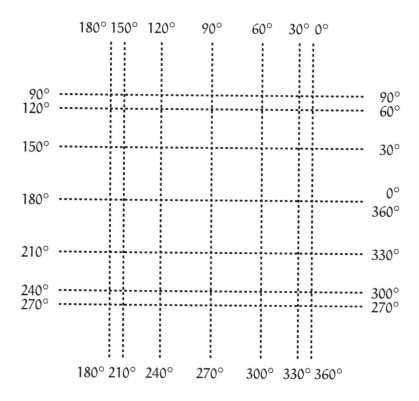

Problems for Chapter 2

Problem 2-1 (Sine and cosine)

Let's compare values of $\cos\theta$ and $\sin\theta$ with 0. In the table below,

- if the value is greater than zero 0, write a "+,"
- if the value equals 0, write a "0," and
- if the value is less than 0 write a "−."

θ	0°	30°	60°	90°	120°	150°
$\cos\theta$	+					
$\sin\theta$	0					

θ	180°	210°	240°	270°	300°	330°
$\cos\theta$	−					
$\sin\theta$	0					

(Answer on page 234)

Problem 2-2 (Lissajous curves)

Use the Lissajous graph template on p. 80 to graph point (x, y) for θ in the range $0° \leqslant \theta < 360°$, as follows:

(1) Point $(x, y) = (\cos(\theta + 30°), \sin(\theta + 30°))$

(2) Point $(x, y) = (\cos\theta, \sin(\theta - 30°))$

(3) Point $(x, y) = (\cos(\theta + 30°), \sin\theta)$

(Answer on page 236)

CHAPTER 3

Around and Around

> "Gather the materials, and I'll create a
> world for you."

3.1 IN THE LIBRARY

While I was doing some math in the library after class one day, Tetra
came up and joined me.

Tetra   "Whatcha working on? Math?"

Me   "You know me."

> Tetra cocks her head to look at what I'm writing.

Tetra   "Is that what it looks like?"

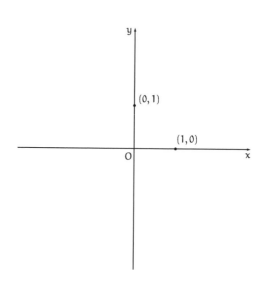

Me "Yep. Just a boring Cartesian plane."

Tetra "But there's nothing on it."

Me "Yeah, I was still just thinking about what I want to do. But there's not *nothing* on it. See the points?"

Tetra "Oh, at $(1,0)$ and $(0,1)$, sure."

Me "That's right, $(1,0)$ on the x-axis, $(0,1)$ on the y-axis. They're important points. You can use them to create a whole world."

Tetra "A whole world from just two points? Must be a pretty small one..."

Me "Hmm, maybe I should have said a whole world in the plane here."

Tetra "Well that's a different story...I guess."

Tetra squints and blinks, looking at the plane.

Me	"Do you understand what it means to say that a figure in a coordinate plane is a set of points?"
Tetra	"Uh, I think so. You mean, like, triangles and circles and lines and stuff, right? And all those are made up of points, so..."
Me	"Sure, that's right. Any figure you could draw on this plane would be a bunch of points. Or a *set* of points, to use the math term."
Tetra	"Right."
Me	"Mathematics uses graphs a lot, and graphs are sets of points. That means that learning how to use points well lets you use graphs well, too."
Tetra	"I see the logic there, but I'm not sure what it means to be able to 'use points well.'"
Me	"Remember when we were playing with the graphs of parabolas a while back, how we thought of parabolas being a set of points?"[1]
Tetra	"Sure, we found equations for those graphs."
Me	"Equations like $y = x^2$, right. And we said that a point on that parabola had to make that equation true."
Tetra	"Sure, the points had to follow a rule if they were going to be on the parabola."
Me	"Exactly. The points have x- and y-values, and when you plug those values into $y = x^2$, you had to get a true statement."
Tetra	"Yeah, I remember all that. So we said that was the graph's equation."

---

[1] See *Math Girls Talk About Equations and Graphs*, Chapter 5.

Me   "Good. So getting back to the coordinate plane, it con-
        tains lots of points. Infinitely many, in fact. In this one
        I've labeled just two, though, $(1, 0)$ and $(0, 1)$."

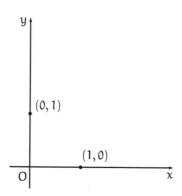

Tetra   "Okay, I understand that—even though you can't see
        them all, this plane is crammed full of points."

Me   "And every point is a pair of numbers. If we write a point
        as (a, b), we're saying that's an x-coordinate a and a y-
        coordinate b."

Tetra   "Yep. I think I first learned that as being like specifying
        the row and column on a checkers board."

Me   "I learned it that way too. But the important thing is
        that it takes two numbers to specify a single point. I was
        thinking about the way we write that, as (a, b). "

Tetra   "Uh...okay?"

Me   "Let me show you. Say that we've picked some point
        (a, b) at random, here."

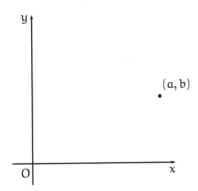

Tetra   "Okay."

Me   "You can see the x- and y- coordinates of this point, right?"

Tetra   "Sure. The x-coordinate is a, and the y-coordinate is b. Like this."

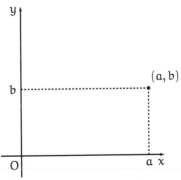

Point (a, b) has an x-component and a y-component

Me   "Perfect. I want to call the a in (a, b) the x-component, and the b the y-component."

Tetra   "Component? Not coordinate?"

Me   "Right, because I'm thinking of a and b as the parts that
            make up the point (a, b)."

Tetra   "Oh, I see."

Me   "It's simple to just write those as a and b, but to really
            understand what those numbers are, we need something
            else—a *unit* for both the x and y directions. We need
            to be clear about how big 1 is, when traveling in each
            direction. I plotted these two points as a way to define
            that."

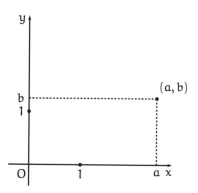

Tetra   "Um...you lost me."

Me   "Like, to get to this point (a, b), you can start at the
            origin and move a to the right, then b up, right?"

Tetra   "Sure."

Me   "But to be sure you wind up at the right place, you have
            to know exactly how far away a is."

Tetra   "Like, some kind of standard, you mean."

Me   "Exactly! That standard is what I'm calling the unit."

Tetra   "Okay, I think I get that."

Me   "So once you've set an origin, and decided where 1 is on the x- and y-axes, you can represent any point in the plane as a pair of numbers, (a, b). Because once you've done all that you've established how far right from the origin you go to hit a, then how far up to get to b."

Tetra   "Like moving right along the squares on a checkerboard, and then up!"

Me   "Except that you won't necessarily be moving by whole squares. Sometimes you only move part of a square, like this."

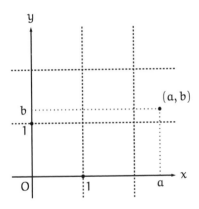

Tetra   "Oh, of course. In this case we move right by 2 and a bit, then up by a little more than 1."

3.2 VECTORS

Me   "All that sums up one way of plotting points in a coordinate plane, but there's another good one. Have you heard of vectors?"

Tetra   "Something about arrows, right? I've heard of them, but I don't really know what they're all about."

Me   "You probably do without realizing it. Everything we've
            been talking about is enough to explain them."

Tetra   "But we haven't drawn any arrows, have we?"

Me   "Not directly. But remember when I said these points
            $(1,0)$ and $(0,1)$ are really important? That's because
            you can use those to define unit vectors."

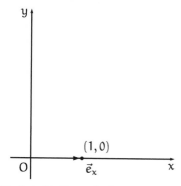

Point $(1,0)$ and the unit vector $\vec{e}_x$

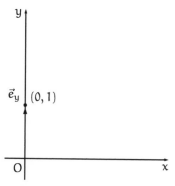

Point $(0,1)$ and the unit vector $\vec{e}_y$

Tetra   "There's those arrows!"

Me   "Yeah, vectors are often drawn using arrows. An arrow between a starting point and some other point."

Tetra   "Pointing at its destination, right?"

Me   "Right. And if you say you're going to fix the starting point at the origin, then the arrow works the same way as these other points we plotted. Because once you've determined a point in the plane, you've also determined where the arrow has to be."

Tetra   "Sure, I guess."

Me   "So the point $(1, 0)$ represents the vector $\vec{e}_x$, and the point $(0, 1)$ represents the vector $\vec{e}_y$. In other words, we can equate points and vectors. We can consider points and vectors as being the same thing."

Tetra   "Oh... yeah?"

Me   "Check out this graph."

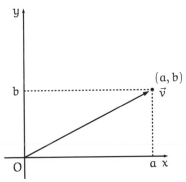

Point (a, b) and vector $\vec{v}$

Me   "What I'm saying is that we can equate this vector $\vec{v}$ and
            this point (a, b)."

Tetra   "I'm sorry, I'm not following all this equating stuff."

Me   "No, I'm probably describing it wrong. It shouldn't be all
            that hard. Anything in particular you're not following?"

Tetra   "Well for starters, why you can think of a vector and a
            point as being the same thing. It seems like there has to
            be, I dunno, some kind of theory behind that."

Me   "Hmm...But it's not like I'm using some kind of deep
            theory to produce a proof here. I'm just talking about a
            different way of looking at things."

            Tetra frowns and crosses her arms.

Me   "I know! Since you like languages, maybe things would
            be clearer if I called vectors a *synonym* for points, an-
            other way of saying the same thing."

Tetra   "So you're like...adding to the vocabulary?"

Me   "Sure, that's a great way to look at it. Before, we had
            two ways of talking about a point on a graph, like this."

- **By graphing**: Directly representing a point by plotting it on
  graph paper

- **By components**: Determining x- and y-axes, and using a
  pair of numbers (a, b) to specify a point's location relative to
  them

Tetra   "Right."

Me   "What I've been talking about is just a third way of
            representing a point."

- **By vectors**: Specifying a point with an arrow whose base is
  at the origin

Tetra   "That's it? Seriously?"

Me   "Seriously. That's the basics, at least. That there's this thing called a vector you can use to specify points, and that you usually draw it as an arrow."

Tetra   "Okay, I guess I'm good then. I just get kind of flustered when I see new math words. It makes everything seem so much harder."

Me   "That happens. Mathematicians sometimes create new words for things, even if they're describing a very simple concept. Doing that makes it easier to say things precisely. I totally understand how unfamiliar words can be confusing, but don't let it get to you. Instead of focusing on the word itself, try to concentrate on the meaning behind it. A lot of the time things aren't as hard as they seem."

3.3 Multiplying Vectors by a Real Number

Tetra   "There's one other thing that's bothering me—why vectors? Aren't normal points good enough?"

Me   "Sure, if you just want to show where a point is. But doing that using vectors lets you pull off some new tricks."

Tetra   "Like what?"

Me   "Like stretch them out. If you multiply a vector by a real number, then you change its length without changing the direction it's pointing in. Like this."

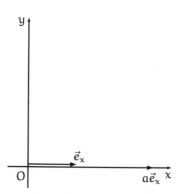

Multiplying the unit vector $\vec{e}_x$ by a real number a

Tetra   "It got longer!"

Me   "Which tells us that $a > 1$. If $0 \leqslant a < 1$, the vector
             would shrink, and if $a < 0$ it would point in the opposite
             direction."

Tetra   "Neat!"

Me   "Here's what happens if you multiply the unit vector $\vec{e}_y$
             by a number a little bit larger than 1."

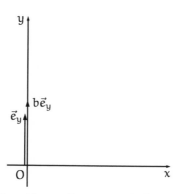

Multiplying the unit vector $\vec{e}_y$ by a real number b

Tetra   "Oh, it grew just a little!"

3.4 ADDING VECTORS

Me   "You can also add vectors together. For example, if we
           added the two vectors we just created, we get this new
           vector $\vec{v}$."

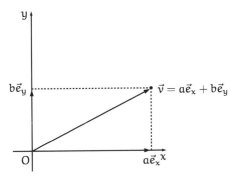

Adding vectors $a\vec{e}_x$ and $b\vec{e}_y$

Tetra   "Wait, I've seen this before! I understood what was going
           on, but I had no idea why I'd ever want to do something
           like that."

Me   "Understandable enough. It's not like adding vectors will
           help you balance a checkbook, or calculate a tip. But
           once you have these two new tools, 'multiplying vectors
           by real numbers' and 'adding vectors,' you can see some-
           thing interesting."

Tetra   "I guess I'm not seeing it yet."

Me   "Well, we have three ways of representing points now,
           right? By plotting them, by thinking of their compo-
           nents, and by using vectors."

Tetra   "Sure."

Me   "When you represent a point as a graph plot, you can see
          exactly where it is. When you think about its compo-
          nents, you know how far right and how far up you have
          to go to get to where it is."

Tetra   "And when you use vectors?"

Me   "You can do calculations using points! Of course you can
          do the same thing using a point's components too, but
          vectors let you ignore them. You can just use the vector
          multiplication and addition we've been talking about."

3.5 ROTATIONS

Tetra   "That kinda makes sense, but it kinda doesn't. I'm still
          not sure what vectors let us do."

Me   "Well, when you came in I was thinking about how we
          could use them to calculate rotations."

Tetra   "Rotations, as in spinning around?"

Me   "Exactly. You need two things to describe a rotation—an
          center of rotation, and an angle of rotation."

Tetra   "The angle of rotation says how far you rotate?"

Me   "That's right, and the center of rotation is the point
          you're rotating around. We'll use the origin $(0, 0)$ for
          that. So we want to rotate a point (a, b) by some angle
          around the origin in the coordinate plane."

Tetra   "Why?"

Me   "Why what?"

Tetra   "Why do we want to rotate a point?"

          I blink and stammer, trying to process this sim-
          plest of questions.

Me   "I mean . . . Like . . . "

Tetra	"Uh oh. I asked a really dumb question again, didn't I."
Me	"No no no, not at all. It's not that. I've just never had to ask myself *why* I'd do things like this."
Tetra	"My math teachers say stuff like that all the time. 'We want to do this-and-that' and 'Let's consider a whatsit' and all, but the first thing I always wonder is why we'd want to do those things. Of course it's all in our textbook too, so I figure what they're talking about is the logical next thing to move on to, but I can never see where we're going, or why we want to go there."

Tetra bites her lip and blushes.

Tetra	"I'm sorry. I'm weird, I know."
Me	"I don't think that's weird at all. But going back to your original question, why we'd want to rotate a point (a, b) in the coordinate plane, I guess the simplest answer is that it's fun to think about things like that."
Tetra	"Fun?"
Me	"Sure. It's sort of like having a toy, but not knowing how you're supposed to play with it. Wouldn't that make you want to touch it, and poke at it, and pull it and twist it and spin it around?"
Tetra	"It would! It totally would!"
Me	"Well math is like that, too. It's the most interesting, most complex toy in the universe."
Tetra	"Wow."
Me	"Some people think like this."

We can use math to manipulate graphs

↓

Graphs are sets of points

↓

Let's mess around with the points and see what happens

"Doesn't that kind of sound like playing with a toy?"

Tetra   "It does!"

Me   "I think that 'I wonder what would happen if...' feeling
          is really important when learning math. There are limits
          to how far you can go with the bare minimum of math
          you have to learn in high school. You've got to push
          beyond that to get to the really fun stuff. Our textbooks
          just give us the basic tools, the ones that are easiest to
          learn and to categorize into classes and lessons. I—"

Tetra   "Whoa!"

Me   "What?"

Tetra   "I just totally realized the difference between you and
          me."

Me   "What would that be?"

Tetra   "To me, math is this thing that's sitting out there, all
          done and waiting for us to learn it. I mean, you flip
          through a textbook and it's right there, laid out and
          organized page by page. But you don't see it that way,
          do you? To you, math is something to play with. I
          think I'm a long way from being able to think of math
          as a toy."

Me   "You might be closer than you think."

Tetra   "How's that?"

Me   "Well, another notebook would be a good start. One
          where you try to remember the math you learned in
          class, and recreate it yourself. That's what I do, at least."

Tetra   "Recreate it? By *myself*?"

Me	"Sure, why not? I've studied rotating points in a plane before, and I think I understand it. But I want to be *sure* I understand it. So today I sat down with an empty notebook, drew some axes and plotted points $(1, 0)$ and $(0, 1)$, and was going to take it from there."
Tetra	"That's way beyond me."
Me	"Then start simple. Try moving a point to the right. Try flipping it over each axis. Anything's fine, so long as you do it on your own. It's your toy. Play with it as much as you want, however you want."
Tetra	"Oh, wow. Well if you put it that way . . ."
Me	"Remember, your goal is to see what you're capable of. That's where you should be starting from, rather than plunging ahead into stuff that's beyond you. That's why I was starting with this empty notebook and two points. I was going to try rotating them when you walked up."
Tetra	"Oops. Guess I interrupted."
Me	"Not at all. I'm more worried about whether you understand why somebody would want to do something like that."
Tetra	"I do! And it even sounds like fun!"

3.6 GRAPHICALLY ROTATING A POINT

Me	"Well let's work on it together, then. First, say we have this point (a, b). We want to rotate it by some angle θ to another point (a', b'). We'll assume that we're rotating to the left, counter-clockwise."
Tetra	"Something like this?"

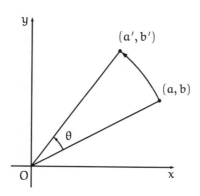

Me   "Exactly. Just like putting the needle of a compass at
          the origin, and drawing an arc."

Tetra   "Gotcha."

Me   "You just rotated a point that's represented as a graph,
          right?"

Tetra   "I did?"

Me   "Sure. We just talked about how we can represent a
          point, yeah? How we can use graphs, or (x, y) compo-
          nents, or vectors..."

Tetra   "Oh, right. Our list of three."

Me   "Well what you drew here is a graphic representation
          of the rotation. What I want to know is, how can we
          represent the rotation using the components of (x, y)?"

Tetra   "Um...okay?"

3.7 Using Coordinates

Me   "I guess that's kinda hard to follow. Let me explain using
          your graph."

Tetra   "Sounds good!"

Me	"We called the point before the rotation (a, b), and the one after the rotation (a', b'), right?"
Tetra	"Right. The point that was here at (a, b) is going *swoop*, over here to (a', b')."
Me	"Since we're representing the point as (a, b), that means the x-coordinate is a, and the y-coordinate is b. You could also say that a is the x-component and b is the y-component."
Tetra	"Gotcha."
Me	"And since we're representing the rotated point as (a', b'), a' is the x-component and b' is the y-component there."
Tetra	"Right. Those are the two numbers for the coordinates after they've swooped."
Me	"So what do you think it means, to rotate a point when it's being represented as an x- and y-coordinate?"
Tetra	"Huh?"
Me	"Maybe I should say, if you're representing a point as x- and y-coordinates, what can you do to those coordinates to rotate the point?"
Tetra	"Oh, I see! But...I don't know."
Me	"How about we think of it this way?"

What it means to rotate a point

'Rotating a point' means using the coordinates $\underline{a}$ and $\underline{b}$ of a non-rotated point (a, b), along with an angle of rotation, to calculate the coordinates $\underline{a'}$ and $\underline{b'}$ of the rotated point (a', b').

Tetra	"Well that makes sense. We take a and b and the angle, and do some kind of complicated calculation, and that will give us a' and b', right?"
Me	"The calculation won't necessarily be complicated, but that's pretty much it. In any case, you're right—we want to use a and b and the angle to calculate a' and b', and if we can do that we'll say that we've rotated the point. Of course, to do the calculating we'll need some kind of equation."
Tetra	"I get all that, but one question."
Me	"You bet."
Tetra	"I'm okay with calculating (a', b') from (a, b), but it sounds like you're only thinking about two points. The one before the rotation and the one after."
Me	"Yeah, sure."
Tetra	"Well what happened to the *swoop*? I mean, when you do this with a compass you're moving from here to there, drawing an arc all the way. Somehow it doesn't feel like a rotation when you warp from one place to another."
Me	"Ah, okay. I see what you're saying, and I totally get why you're uncomfortable calling this a rotation. But in this case we only need to worry about the two points."
Tetra	"Why's that?"
Me	"Because the rotation we're going to do uses trig functions."
Tetra	"Oh. Hmm."
Me	"We're using the letter θ to name the angle of rotation, which makes this a case of generalization through the use of variables."
Tetra	"Ooh, that's good. Hang on."

Tetra writes this in the notebook she's been using
to keep track of her new math discoveries.

Tetra   "So what we're generalizing is a rotation by some angle θ,
             right?"

Me   "Right, and that means that once we're done you'll be
             able to set θ to any value you like. You'll even be able
             to swoop if you want, sorta, in small jumps."

. Tetra   "Because I can use tiny little angles to move from a to
             b!"

Me   "Exactly. That way once you can use a letter to gen-
             eralize the angle, you can just give any two points and
             approximate the arc between them."

Tetra   "Got it. Now we just need to find that equation that
             does the rotating!"

Me   "Sounds like an excellent next step."

3.8 Our Problem

Me   "Let's start out by thinking about the problem we've set
             for ourselves."

Our problem: We want to rotate point (a, b)

- We'll use the origin $(0, 0)$ as the center of rotation.

- We'll name the angle of rotation θ.

- We'll call the point to rotate (a, b).

- We'll call the point after rotation (a', b').

Given the above, use a, b, and θ to represent a' and b'.

Tetra   "Umm, I'm totally clear on what the problem is, but . . . I
             have no idea how to find the answer."

Me   "That's nothing to be ashamed of. You've never done
             this, so there's no reason why you should see the answer
             right off the bat."

Tetra   "Could you show me?"

Me   "I could, but even better would be to work though it
             together. That way I can show you what I do when I'm
             not sure how to apply math to a problem."

Tetra   "Like, your thought process when you're working prob-
             lems? I'd love to see that!"

Me   "Well I hope I don't make a fool of myself, then. Anyway,
             we're trying to solve the general problem of rotating a
             point (a, b) by some angle θ—"

Tetra points at the most recent line in her notebook.

Tetra   "Using generalization through the use of variables!"

Me   "Right. The problem is, while it's important to think in
             general terms, it's kinda hard to think that abstractly.
             So it's often better to start out in the other direction, and
             think of special situations, concrete cases. Specialization
             through assignment to a variable, if you like."

Tetra   "Huh?"

3.9 A Point on the x-axis

Me   "For example, instead of thinking about *any* point (a, b),
             let's start out thinking about a point on the x-axis.
             We're limiting the possibilities to just a point on the
             x-axis, in other words."

Tetra   "That's an example of 'specialization through assignment to a variable'?"

Me   "It is. Because saying the point has to be on the x-axis means the y-coordinate has to be 0. So we're assigning 0 to the b in point (a, b), and only thinking of the point $(a, 0)$ instead. Hopefully that will make the problem easier to start."

Tetra   "That would be nice!"

Me   "So here's a new problem."

Problem 1: Rotating a point $(a, 0)$ on the x-axis

- We'll use the origin $(0, 0)$ as the center of rotation.

- We'll name the angle of rotation θ.

- We'll call the point to rotate $(a, 0)$.

- We'll call the point after rotation (a_1, b_1).

Given the above, use a and θ to represent a_1 and b_1.

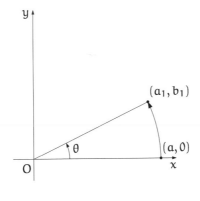

Tetra looks back and forth, comparing this problem with the previous one.

Tetra   "The b is gone!"

Me   "Yep, our specialization got rid of a variable. That's why
         I'm hoping this will make things easier."

Tetra   "Do you think I could solve this one?"

Me   "The first step toward finding out would be to graph
         that, by yourself."

Tetra   "Good idea!"

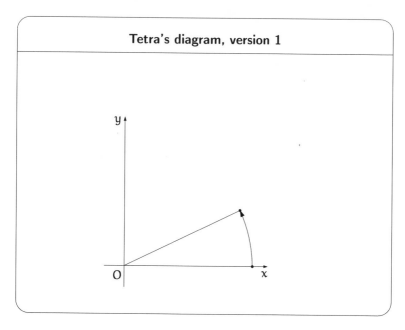

Tetra's diagram, version 1

Tetra   "Done!"

Me   "What are you looking for?"

Tetra   "Huh?"

Me	"That's a question you always need to ask yourself when you're doing math. In this problem, what exactly are you trying to find?"
Tetra	"Um... a_1 and b_1?"
Me	"Then those need to be in your graph."
Tetra	"Oh, good point!"

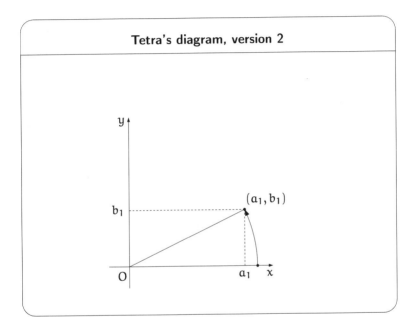

Tetra's diagram, version 2

Me	"Still not enough to solve the problem, though."
Tetra	"No?"
Me	"There's another question you always need to ask yourself: what information have you been given?"
Tetra	"I've been given... oh, a! Because b is gone now."
Me	"Just a?"
Tetra	"Oops! Also the angle θ. I'm given a and θ."

Me	"So again, those should be in your graph."
Tetra	"Oh, yeah. You're right."
Me	"Something bothering you?"
Tetra	"Your questions."

- What are you trying to find?
- What information have you been given?

"I guess they just made me realize how flighty I am. I just read problems without thinking much about them, and draw graphs without really thinking about what I'm doing. I need to learn to ask myself these questions, and think about what I'm doing, and why."

Me	"You'll definitely find it helpful when you're doing hard problems."
Tetra	"Well, anyway, third time's the charm!"

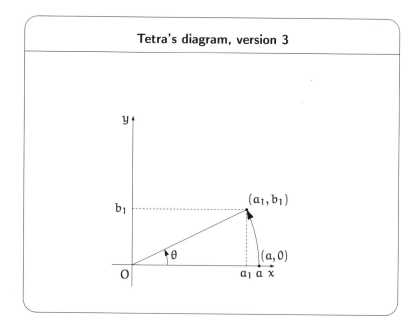

Tetra's diagram, version 3

Me   "Good. Now on with the problem. Here's what we have
          so far."

- What do we want to solve for? a_1 and b_1.

- What information have we been given? a and θ.

Me   "Any idea what to do next?"

Tetra   "Well...Hmm..."

Me   "We're actually getting pretty close.   Maybe another
          question will help: have you seen something similar be-
          fore?"

Tetra   "Similar to this? Uh...I don't think so."

Me   "Here's a big hint."

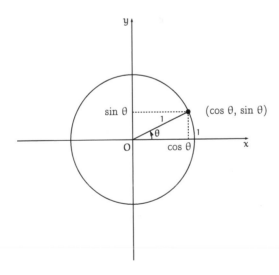

The relation between the unit circle, $\cos\theta$, and $\sin\theta$

Tetra   "Isn't this the graph we used to define the sine function?"

Me   "It is indeed. Doesn't it look kinda similar to the graph
             you drew to solve this Problem 1, if we draw the whole
             circle?"

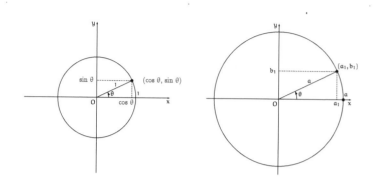

Tetra   "Oh, wow! They're practically identical! I guess the only
             difference is that the radius of the left circle is 1, and the
             radius on the right is a. Does that mean...?"

Me   "Go ahead. Does that mean what?"

Tetra   "Well, just a guess, but does that mean we need to multi-
             ply stuff by a? The x-coordinate and the y-coordinate?"

Me   "Excellent. Yes, it does. So how would you write that as
             an equation?"

Tetra   "If we have to multiply both by a, something like this?"

$$\begin{cases} a_1 = a\cos\theta & \text{multiply x-coord. of a point on the unit circle by } a \\ b_1 = a\sin\theta & \text{multiply y-coord. of a point on the unit circle by } a \end{cases}$$

Me   "Perfect!"

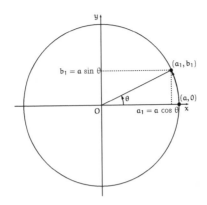

Tetra   "Yeah? Wow, I'm surprised it was that simple!"

Me   "What works, works."

Tetra   "I guess so."

Me   "Now, take a close look at these two equations you've found."

$$\begin{cases} a_1 &= a \cos \theta \\ b_1 &= a \sin \theta \end{cases}$$

Tetra   "What am I looking for?"

Me   "Try looking past the cosine and sine. See how you've found a_1 and b_1 from a and θ?"

Tetra   "Hey, yeah! And that's what we wanted to do! Solve for a_1 and b_1 in terms of a and θ!"

Me   "That's right."

Tetra   "Just to be sure, did I write that correctly? Is it $a \cos \theta$ and $a \sin \theta$?"

Me   "Sure. Why?"

Tetra	"Just wanted to be sure that's how you show multiplying a and $\cos\theta$."
Me	"You're right. If it's less confusing, you can think of $\cos\theta$ the way you think of other functions, putting the argument in parentheses."

$$\begin{cases} a\cos\theta & = a \times \cos(\theta) \\ a\sin\theta & = a \times \sin(\theta) \end{cases}$$

Tetra	"Good, that makes it much clearer."
Me	"Anyway, now you're done. You've solved problem 1."

Solution to Problem 1: Rotating a point $(a, 0)$ on the x-axis

- We'll use the origin $(0, 0)$ as the center of rotation.

- We'll name the angle of rotation θ.

- We'll call the point to rotate $(a, 0)$.

- We'll call the point after rotation (a_1, b_1).

Given the above, we can use a and θ to represent a_1 and b_1 as follows:

$$\begin{cases} a_1 & = a\cos\theta \\ b_1 & = a\sin\theta \end{cases}$$

Tetra	"Let's be honest—you did more solving than I did. But still..."
Me	"Still?"
Tetra	"Even if I did need plenty of hints it feels great to have been able to work through this. It seemed so impossible at first."
Me	"That's one of the best feelings you can have when doing math."

3.10 A POINT ON THE y-AXIS

Me   "Let's see if you can do it again, with fewer hints this
          time. Here's problem 2."

Problem 2: Rotating a point $(0, b)$ on the y-axis

- We'll use the origin $(0, 0)$ as the center of rotation.

- We'll name the angle of rotation θ.

- We'll call the point to rotate $(0, b)$.

- We'll call the point after rotation (a_2, b_2).

Given the above, use b and θ to represent a_2 and b_2.

Me   "Give it a shot."

Tetra   "By myself? I don't know if I can do that . . ."

Me   "You absolutely can. I guarantee it."

Miruka   "Guarantee what?"

Tetra   "Hey, Miruka!"

Miruka glanced down at our graphs.

Miruka   "Hmph. Rotations, huh?"

Tetra   "Not just that, though. Problem solving in general."

- What are you trying to find?

- What information have you been given?

- Have you seen something similar before?

Miruka   "That'd be Pólya."

Me   "I should've known you'd recognize it."

Tetra   "What's a Pólya?"

Miruka   "A mathematician who wrote a bestseller called *How to Solve It*.[2] Good book. It's filled with hints about how to study math and solve problems."

Me   "These questions I'm making you answer are straight out of that book, in fact."

Tetra   "I'll be sure to check it out!"

An excerpt from Pólya's list

- What is the unknown?

- What are the data?

- Draw a diagram, using appropriate symbols.

- Do you know a related problem?

Me   "So anyway, let's get back to problem 2."

Tetra   "Oh, right!"

Tetra struggles for a while, but manages to solve the problem and produce a graph.

---

[2]Princeton University Press, 1944

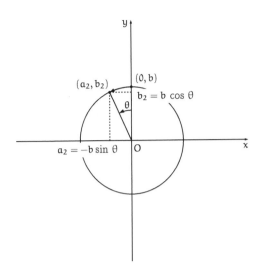

Rotating a point $(0, b)$ on the y-axis

Tetra   "I think I got it! I like this 'what are you looking for' and 'what are you given' stuff!"

Solution to Problem 2: Rotating a point $(0, b)$ on the y-axis

- We'll use the origin $(0, 0)$ as the center of rotation.

- We'll name the angle of rotation θ.

- We'll call the point to rotate $(0, b)$.

- We'll call the point after rotation (a_2, b_2).

Given the above, we can use b and θ to represent a_2 and b_2 as follows:

$$\begin{cases} a_2 & = -b \sin \theta \\ b_2 & = b \cos \theta \end{cases}$$

Me   "Good job! You didn't even get the sine and cosine functions confused! Let's compare this with problem 1."

Problem 1 solution   **Problem 2 solution**

$$\begin{cases} a_1 &= a\cos\theta \\ b_1 &= a\sin\theta \end{cases} \qquad \begin{cases} a_2 &= -b\sin\theta \\ b_2 &= b\cos\theta \end{cases}$$

Tetra   "Yeah, I noticed that the sine and cosine functions get flipped. And one gets a minus sign, too. Everything's pretty easy to see if you tilt your head 90° to the left."

Tetra flops her head over and peers at the graph.

Me   "Maybe most people would just rotate the paper instead?"

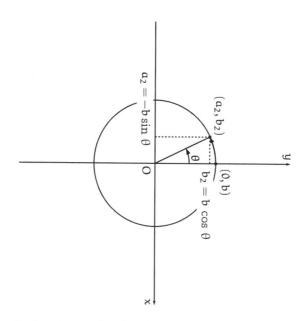

A graph showing point $(0, b)$ rotated, turned 90° clockwise

Tetra   "Oh, yeah, sure. Anyway, that's how I solved it."

Miruka   "Hmph."

Me   "So look what you have now, Tetra. You rotated a point $(a, 0)$ to (a_1, b_1), and a point $(0, b)$ to (a_2, b_2), right?"

Tetra   "Right."

Me   "So you solved two point rotation problems."

Tetra   "I guess."

Me   "Time for a new question: can you apply these results?"

Miruka   "More Pólya."

Tetra   "Apply them? Use them in another problem, you mean?"

Me   "Exactly."

Tetra   "Uh...what other problem?"

Me   "The original problem we started working on. Rotating *any* point, not just one on an axis."

Our problem: We want to rotate point (a, b)

- We'll use the origin $(0, 0)$ as the center of rotation.
- We'll name the angle of rotation θ.
- We'll call the point to rotate (a, b).
- We'll call the point after rotation (a', b').

Given the above, use a, b, and θ to represent a' and b'.

Tetra   "Oh, right. Hmm, let's see..."

Miruka   "If Pólya were here, he'd be telling you to draw a graph."

Me   "No doubt."

Tetra   "Okay, I'll try that."

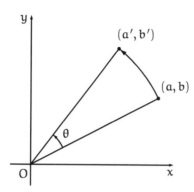

Point (a, b) rotated by θ to point (a', b')

Miruka   "I see a rotating rectangle hidden in there."

Tetra   "A rectangle? Where?"

Miruka   "Like this."

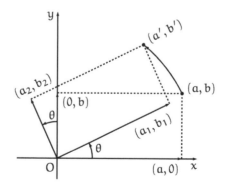

The hidden rotated rectangle

Me   "And I see a vector addition problem hidden in that."

Tetra   "Vectors too?"

Miruka   "A parallelogram, if you're going to use arrows in the general case, but here it's the diagonal of a rectangle. As coordinates, it's a sum of corresponding elements."

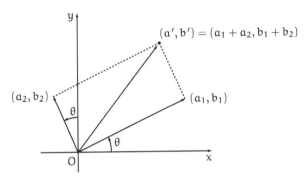

The hidden vector addition

Tetra   "Er...Uh..."

Miruka   "Tetra's already found (a_1, b_1) and (a_2, b_2)."

Me   "She has."

Tetra   "I have, but..."

Me   "Oh, and that's all she needs to solve the problem."

> ### Our problem: We want to rotate point (a, b)
>
> - We'll use the origin $(0, 0)$ as the center of rotation.
>
> - We'll name the angle of rotation θ.
>
> - We'll call the point to rotate (a, b).
>
> - We'll call the point after rotation (a', b').
>
> Given the above, we can use a, b, and θ to represent a' and b' as follows:
>
> $$\begin{cases} a' & = a_1 + a_2 = a \cos\theta - b \sin\theta \\ b' & = b_1 + b_2 = a \sin\theta + b \cos\theta \end{cases}$$

Tetra   "Ack. So many letters."

Me   "Take your time with it. Look at your solutions to the other two problems to see where the complex parts of the equation are coming from. And remember that (a', b') is coming from (a_1, b_1) and (a_2, b_2)."

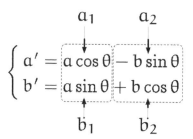

Tetra looks back and forth between the graphs we've drawn.

Miruka   "Let's move on to rotation matrices already."

Me   "Yeah, that would be fun! It's so cool that just thinking about rotating points leads to vectors and trig functions and matrices... all kinds of things."

| Miruka | "Don't forget complex numbers." |

| Me | "Right! Oh, and also—" |

| Tetra | "Whoa, guys, slow down! You're losing me!" |

| Me | "You look a little pale, Tetra." |

| Tetra | "It's just...You guys know so much. Elements and planes and vectors and Pólya and matrices and just...everything! You mention something I've never heard of and she comes back with some other thing I don't know, then back to you and around and around...It's all kind of overwhelming sometimes." |

| Miruka | "It's love." |

| Tetra | "Oh. Oh, I see." |

| Me | "Uh, I don't know if I'd go *that* far. I mean we hardly... We haven't even..." |

Miruka cocks an eyebrow at me.

| Miruka | "I'm talking about how much we love math. What are you going on about?" |

| Me | "Urgh. I...uh—" |

Ms. Mizutani "The library is *closed!*"

The school librarian's announcement killed any hope of talking about rotation matrices that day, but I was relieved nonetheless. I walked home that day wondering what trials and odd turns of fate awaited us as we explored the new worlds opening up to us.

"But what's the difference between creating a world, and gathering the materials to do so?"

Problems for Chapter 3

Problem 3-1 (Rotating points)

Taking

- the origin $(0, 0)$ as the center of rotation,

- θ as the angle of rotation, and

- $(1, 0)$ as the starting point,

find the point (x, y) after the rotation.

(Answer on page 238)

Problem 3-2 (Rotating points)

Taking

- the origin $(0, 0)$ as the center of rotation,

- θ as the angle of rotation, and

- $(0, 1)$ as the starting point,

find the point (x, y) after the rotation.

(Answer on page 238)

Problem 3-3 (Rotating points)

Taking

- the origin $(0, 0)$ as the center of rotation,

- θ as the angle of rotation, and

- $(1, 1)$ as the starting point,

find the point (x, y) after the rotation.

(Answer on page 239)

Problem 3-4 (Rotating points)

Taking

- the origin $(0,0)$ as the center of rotation,

- θ as the angle of rotation, and

- (a, b) as the starting point,

find the point (x, y) after the rotation.

(Answer on page 239)

CHAPTER **4**

Calculating Pi

> "When the world sees something for
> the first time, it's a big deal."

4.1 IN MY ROOM

Yuri   "I am *sooo booored.* Entertain me."

Me   "What, you didn't bring anything fun?"

Yuri   "What would I bring?"

Me   "I dunno. Magic tricks. Puzzle boxes. That kind of thing."

Yuri   "Fresh out. You were my last hope."

Me   "Sorry to disappoint. Grab a book and entertain yourself."

Yuri   "I see you still haven't learned anything about how to treat girls."

Me   "Whatever."

Yuri	"C'mon c'mon c'mon! Think of something!"
Me	"I suppose I won't get any peace until I do. Let's see..."
Yuri	"...Well?"
Me	"I know. How about calculating pi?"

4.2 Pi

Me	"Have you ever heard of pi?"
Yuri	"Have you ever heard of giraffes?"
Me	"Of course. Why?"
Yuri	"Oh, I thought we were playing the stupid question game."
Me	"Seriously, when you're doing math it's important to verify definitions. Using words you don't totally understand will lead to all kinds of trouble."
Yuri	"I'm pretty sure I know what pi is, though. It's just 3.14, right?"
Me	"Yes... and no."
Yuri	"Yeah, yeah. And it goes on forever. 3.14-whatever-whatever-whatever."
Me	"Still, yes and no."
Yuri	"What part of that is no?"
Me	"You're right that pi goes on forever, $3.141592653589793\cdots$ and on and on. But that's not the *definition* of pi."
Yuri	"That's what I learned it as."
Me	"What you're describing is the *value* of pi. The definition has to be something like 'pi is defined as the value derived from the something-something.'"

Yuri   "Then can't you just say 'pi is defined as the value 3.14···' ?"

Me   "But if you do it that way you don't know what pi *is*, other than being a number."

Yuri   "Hmm... Sounds like one of those nitpicky math things."

Me   "Have you heard the phrase 'pi is the ratio of the circumference of a circle to its diameter' ?"

Yuri   "Now that you mention it..."

Me   "So pi is the answer to a division problem, circumference divided by diameter. I'm saying we should check for ourselves what that value is. And while we're at it, we should make sure that when we divide the circumference of *any* circle by its diameter, we always get the same number."

Definition of pi (π)

Pi is the ratio of the circumference of a circle to its diameter. In other words,

$$\pi = \text{circumference} \div \text{diameter}.$$

Yuri   "But pi really does equal 3.14···, and so on and so on, right?"

Me   "It does."

Yuri   "And the diameter of a circle is its radius doubled, right?"

Me   "Sure. So if you want, you could define pi using the circumference and radius instead."

Another definition of pi

Let ℓ be the circumference of a circle, and let r be its radius. Then pi is defined as

$$\pi = \frac{\ell}{2r}.$$

ℓ

r

Yuri   "Got it. This is the same pi you use to find the circumference, right?"

Me   "Right. You probably did that using pi and the radius."

Finding the circumference of a circle from its radius

Let r be the radius of a circle, and let π be the ratio of a circle's circumference to its diameter. Then the circumference ℓ of the circle is

$$\ell = 2\pi r.$$

ℓ

r

4.3 THE AREA OF A CIRCLE

Me   "When you did all this in class, did you also use pi to calculate the areas of circles?"

Yuri   "Yep. The area is πr^2, right? Pi times the radius times the radius."

Me   "That's the one."

Finding the area of a circle from its radius

Let r be the radius of a circle, and let π be the ratio of a circle's circumference to its diameter. Then the area S of the circle is

$$S = \pi r^2.$$

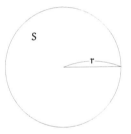

Yuri   "So getting back to your alleged entertainment, what do you mean by calculating pi?"

Me   "Well, to do that, let's first take a closer look at this area formula."

$$S = \pi r^2$$

Yuri   "Okay, I'm looking. Closely."

Me   "This formula lets you calculate the area of a circle from its radius, right?"

Yuri	"Right."
Me	"Let's see what happens when we move things around a bit."

$$S = \pi r^2 \qquad \text{formula for the area of a circle}$$
$$\pi r^2 = S \qquad \text{swap left and right sides}$$
$$\pi = \frac{S}{r^2} \qquad \text{divide both sides by } r^2$$

Yuri	"Er, what happened?"
Me	"We got an equation like this."

$$\pi = \frac{S}{r^2}$$

Yuri	"And?"
Me	"In this equation, S is the area of a circle, and r is its radius, right?"
Yuri	"Yeah? So?"
Me	"Well that means if you know a circle's area and radius, you can use $\pi = \frac{S}{r^2}$ to calculate pi!"
Yuri	"Wow! That's... probably really cool. What does it mean?"
Me	"Just what I said. If you can find the area of a circle and the length of its radius with enough precision, you can use that information to calculate pi."
Yuri	"Yeah, wow, neat. Hmm, I wonder if there's anything good on TV ..."
Me	"Oh, come on. It'll be fun. Think of the look on your classmates' faces when you tell them you calculated pi all by yourself."

Yuri	"Out of morbid curiosity, what did your friends say?"
Me	"Huh?"
Yuri	"When you announced to your class that you'd mastered pi, that you'd confirmed it was 3.14 whatever whatever, how did they react?"
Me	"Er, well..."
Yuri	"Well?"
Me	"I've never actually, uh..."
Yuri	"Are you trying to tell me you've never done this before?"
Me	"Actually, no."
Yuri	"But you were going to try to make me do it, while you sit back and watch? Hey, who's entertaining who here?"
Me	"Okay, okay. We'll do it together."
Yuri	"You bet we will. And I warn you, this had better be fun."

4.4 ESTIMATING PI

Yuri	"So where do we start?"
Me	"By approximating, doing something like this."

A method for approximating pi

Step 1. Use a compass to draw a circle with radius r on graph paper.

Step 2. Count the number of squares inside the circle. Call the number of squares n.

Step 3. Calculate pi using r and n as $\frac{n}{r^2}$.

Yuri   "Sounds easy enough. Let's get to it."

Me   "Hang on, let me explain some stuff first."

Yuri   "Gah, your explanations take too much time."

Me   "It's important, though. We have to be sure we know
          what we're doing."

          Yuri sighs.

Yuri   "Get on with it, then."

Me   "No problem with step 1, right? We just use a compass
          to draw a circle with radius r."

Yuri   "So how long should r be?"

Me   "Hmm..."

Yuri   "Oh, right. You've never done this before."

Me   "Let's start with $r = 10$. Ten squares on the graph paper,
          I mean."

Yuri   "Fair enough."

Me   "The next step says we have to count the number of
          squares in the circle, and call that number n. Since we'll
          only count squares that are inside the circle, n will be a
          little less than the area S."

Yuri   "Things are starting to sound a bit fuzzy."

Me   "They are, but necessary for the last step, calculating
          $\frac{n}{r^2}$."

Yuri   "Where did that come from again?"

Me   "Because the area of a circle is $S = \pi r^2$. Remember how
          we used that to get $\pi = \frac{S}{r^2}$?"

Yuri   "Right, right. Carry on."

Me   "Finding an accurate value of pi would require accurate
            values for the area S and the radius r. We aren't being
            very accurate when we use n instead of the true value
            of S, and calculating pi using $\frac{n}{r^2}$ instead of $\frac{S}{r^2}$. But
            n approximates S, so it's good enough to give us an
            approximate value of pi."

Yuri   "Got it. Can we get started now?"

4.5 A CIRCLE WITH RADIUS 10

I draw a circle with a compass.

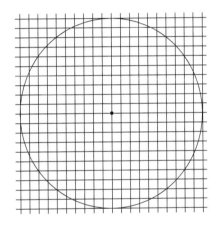

Me   "I guess that should do it for step 1."

Yuri   "That has a radius of 10?"

Me   "Of 10 side-lengths of our squares, yeah. So its diameter
            is 20. On to step 2."

Yuri   "Now we have to count the number of squares in the
            circle, right?"

Me   "Right. That gives us n, which we're using in place of
            the true area."

Yuri	"Okay. One, two, three ..."
Me	"Hang on, you need to mark the squares as you count them."
Yuri	"Sounds like you think I make mistakes."
Me	"C'mon, Yuri. Let's do it right."
Yuri	"Fine, fine ... Hey, what do we do about the ones on the edge?"
Me	"What do you mean?"
Yuri	"These squares that the circle passes through. Do we count those?"

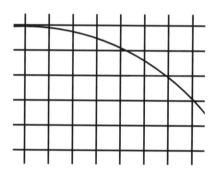

| Me | "We should really keep track of both. Let's color squares that are completely inside the circle light gray, and ones that are on the circumference dark gray." |

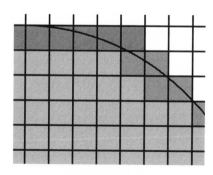

Yuri   "Got it. Wow, there's a lot of squares here. Gonna be a pain to count— Oh!"

Me   "Oh what?"

Yuri   "We don't have to count all of them! We can just count half of them, then double!"

Me   "Good idea!"

Yuri   "I know."

Me   "But even better, we can just count the squares in the upper right quadrant, and multiply that by 4."

Yuri   "Yeah, I guess that works too. Okay, here goes... And, finished!"

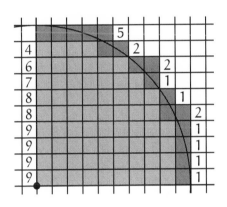

Me   "Nicely done. These numbers are the counts across, right? The number of light gray squares in the interior, and the number of dark gray squares on the circumference?"

Yuri   "Well, one-fourth of those numbers, if you're thinking of the whole circle."

Me   "Okay, then let's do some adding and see what we get."

$$4 + 6 + 7 + 8 \times 2 + 9 \times 4 = 69$$

Me   "Okay, 69 here. So there's four times that in the whole circle. That's our n value."

$$n = \text{number of light gray squares} \times 4$$
$$= 69 \times 4$$
$$= 276 \quad \text{squares in a circle of radius 10}$$

Yuri   "And we can use this to calculate pi?"

Me   "Well, we're using n in place of S, so we have to use $\frac{n}{r^2}$ in place of $\frac{S}{r^2}$. What we should end up with is something a little bit less than the true value of pi."

$$
\begin{aligned}
\text{A number slightly smaller than pi} &= \frac{n}{r^2} \\
&= \frac{276}{r^2} \quad \text{because } n = 276 \\
&= \frac{276}{10^2} \quad \text{because } r = 10 \\
&= \frac{276}{100} \\
&= 2.76
\end{aligned}
$$

Yuri   "2.76!? That's not even 3, and forget about 3.14!"

Me   "No, but at least it's a slightly smaller number, as we predicted."

Yuri   "You're one of those glass-half-full guys, aren't you?"

Me   "Let's try it again, this time including the dark gray squares we excluded before. Then the area should be a little too large, so we should get a number slightly larger than pi."

Yuri   "Let's see... 5 dark gray squares here, then 2, and 2, and two 1s, and another 2, then four more 1s..."

$$5 + 2 + 2 + 1 \times 2 + 2 + 1 \times 4 = 17$$

Me   "And that's for one-fourth of the entire circle, so we need to multiply that 17 by 4. And here's what we get."

$$\text{A number slightly larger than pi} = \frac{n + \text{number of dark gray squares} \times 4}{r^2}$$

$$= \frac{n + 17 \times 4}{r^2}$$

$$= \frac{276 + 17 \times 4}{r^2}$$

$$= \frac{276 + 68}{r^2}$$

$$= \frac{344}{r^2}$$

$$= \frac{344}{10^2}$$

$$= \frac{344}{100}$$

$$= 3.44$$

Yuri   "3.44, huh? Yep, we overshot it this time."

Me   "Let's summarize what we have so far, based on counting
            squares."

A range for pi based on a circle with radius 10

$$2.76 < \pi < 3.44$$

The true value of pi should be larger than 2.76 and smaller than
3.44.

Me   "So we haven't gotten an exact value, but at least we've
            found a range—we're looking for a number somewhere
            between 2.76, which we found by just counting the light
            gray squares, and 3.44, which we got from also counting
            the dark gray squares."

Yuri   "There's something not very satisfying about that. The
            range is too wide."

Me   "I agree."

Yuri   "It seems like we should be able to get a lot closer than
            this. Why the huge spread?"

Me   "Why do you think?"

Yuri   "Because we're working too...roughly?"

Me   "How do you mean?"

Yuri   "Well, look how ziggedy zaggedy everything is. It's all
            corners, not round."

Me   "You're right. And pi is all about circles."

Yuri   "We need to get rounder...Hey, I know! We can add
            more squares!"

Me   "Good idea. More squares would give us a larger r."

Yuri   "Let's try $r = 100$!"

Me   "That would be...challenging. How about $r = 50$ in-
            stead?"

Yuri   "Fair enough."

4.6 A CIRCLE WITH RADIUS 50

Me   "Done?"

Yuri   "Well, I drew the circle at least. But there's so many
            squares..."

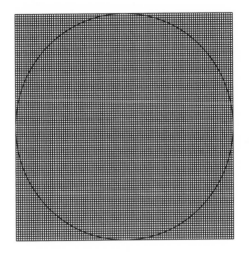

Me   "Well, we can try counting just one-eighth of them this
            time, but it's still going to be some work."

Yuri   "No use putting it off, I guess."

            Yuri begins counting, and I thumb through a book
            until she raises her head.

Me   "Done?"

Yuri   "I am!"

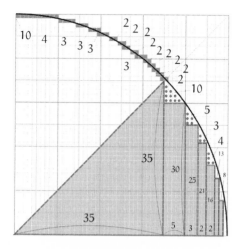

Me   "Okay, read off the number of squares on the circumfer-
            ence in this half quadrant, and I'll tally them up."

Yuri   "There's 10, then 4, then four 3s and nine 2s."

One-eighth circumference $= 10 + 4 + 3 \times 4 + 2 \times 9 = 44$

Me   "That adds up to 44, so the circumference is $44 \times 8 =$
            352."

Yuri   "Oh, and I figured out a faster way of counting the
            squares inside the circle. See?"

Me   "Using a triangle and some rectangles. Well done."

Yuri   "The triangle is half of a 35 by 35 square, and the rect-
            angles are 5×30, 3×25, 2×21, 2×16, 1×13, and 1×8.
            That leaves these areas up here, which have 10, 5, 3, and
            4 squares."

$$\text{Triangle} = \frac{35 \times 35}{2} = 612.5$$

$$\text{Rectangles} = 5 \times 30 + 3 \times 25 + 2 \times 21 + 2 \times 16 + 1 \times 13 + 1 \times 8$$

$$= 150 + 75 + 42 + 32 + 13 + 8$$

$$= 320$$

$$\text{Gaps} = 10 + 5 + 3 + 4$$

$$= 22$$

$$\text{Total} = 612.5 + 320 + 22$$

$$= 954.5$$

Me   "So one-eighth of the circle has 954.5 squares, and the whole circle has $954.5 \times 8 = 7636$."

Yuri   "And we can use that to do a better calculation?"

Me   "Yep. The radius is 50, and there are 7636 squares if we only count the interior, and $7636 + 352 = 7988$ squares if we also count ones on the circumference."

Yuri   "So r^2 is 50×50, which is... 2500!"

$$\text{A number slightly smaller than pi} = \frac{7636}{2500}$$

$$= 3.0544$$

$$\text{A number slightly larger than pi} = \frac{7636 + 352}{2500}$$

$$= \frac{7988}{2500}$$

$$= 3.1952$$

Me   "Here's what we end up with."

> **A range for pi based on a circle with radius** 50
>
> $$3.0544 < \pi < 3.1952$$
>
> The true value of pi should be larger than 3.0544 and smaller than 3.1952.

Yuri   "Hmm..."

Me   "Hmm..."

Yuri   "You know what I'm thinkin'?"

Me   "What's that?"

Yuri   "That we aren't quite there yet."

Me   "I've gotta agree."

Yuri   "After all that work, I want to see a 3.14!"

Me   "Well, at least we're closing in on it."

Yuri   "How's that?"

Me   "Our range is a lot narrower now. See?"

$$3.44 - 2.76 = 0.68 \qquad \text{range when } r = 10$$
$$3.1952 - 3.0544 = 0.1408 \qquad \text{range when } r = 50$$

Yuri   "From 0.68 to 0.1408, huh. Not bad, I guess, but I remain unfulfilled."

4.7 REFINING PI

Me	"Where do you want to go from here?"
Yuri	"What do you mean?"
Me	"Do you want to leave things like this? With having found pi to be some number between 3.0544 and 3.1952?"
Yuri	"No way I'm going to admit defeat! I ain't leaving here until I see a 3.14."
Me	"Want to try a bigger r?"
Yuri	"There's got to be a better way. C'mon, think of something! Think, think!"
Me	"Stop shaking the table like that."
Yuri	"*Think!*"
Me	"I'm thinking, I'm thinking..."

4.8 ARCHIMEDES' METHOD

Me	"Okay, enough with counting squares. Let's try Archimedes' method."
Yuri	"What's that?"
Me	"It's a way of estimating pi using regular polygons. Here's an example using hexagons."

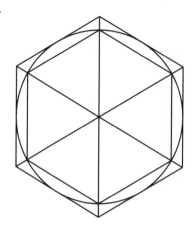

Me   "See the two hexagons?"

Yuri   "Sure, one snuggling up inside the circle, and one hugging
            it from the outside."

Me   "Right. A polygon with its vertices on a circle is called an
            inscribed polygon. One with a circle inside that touches
            each of its sides is called a circumscribed polygon. We
            want to calculate some number that's close to pi, by
            finding a tight range that it must be in. Archimedes'
            method does that using this inequality."

$$\begin{array}{ccc} \text{circumference of an} \\ \text{inscribed } n\text{-gon} \end{array} < \begin{array}{c} \text{circumference} \\ \text{of a circle} \end{array} < \begin{array}{c} \text{circumference of a} \\ \text{circumscribed } n\text{-gon} \end{array}$$

Yuri   "What's an n-gon?"

Me   "A polygon with n sides. So you could also call a hexagon
            a 6-gon, for example."

Yuri   "Ah, I get it. The circumference of the circle has to be
            something between the circumference of the inside and
            outside whatever-gons."

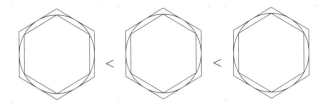

Me   "Exactly. Come to think of it, we can make the calcu-
            lations a little easier by doubling everything. Let's call
            the circumference of an inscribed n-gon $2L_n$, and the
            circumference of a circumscribed n-gon $2M_n$. So for a
            hexagon, where $n = 6$, we get this."

$$2L_6 < 2\pi < 2M_6$$

Yuri   "I'm totally not seeing how that makes things easier."

Me   "In this case $2L_6$ is the circumference of an inscribed
            hexagon, $2M_6$ is the circumference of a circumscribed
            hexagon, and the 2π in the middle is the circumference
            of a circle with radius 1. Because the circumference of a
            circle is $2\pi r$, so when $r = 1$ we just get 2π."

Yuri   "Why do we want all these 2s?"

Me   "So that we can get rid of them, by dividing through by
            a 2."

$$L_6 < \pi < M_6$$

Me   "Now we've got π trapped between L_6 and M_6."

Yuri   "Where does that get us?"

Me   "Well, Archimedes went from using hexagons to do-
            decagons next."

Yuri   "How many gons is that?"

Me   "Twelve."

Yuri   "So he went from 6 to 12 . . . Oh, he doubled."

Me	"Right. And the regular 12-gons will fit between the circle and the 6-gons, so we get this."

$$L_6 < \underline{L_{12}} < \pi < \underline{M_{12}} < M_6$$

Yuri	" ... Oh!"
Me	"See where this is going?"
Yuri	"Maybe."
Me	"What was trapped between L_6 and M_6 is now trapped between L_{12} and M_{12}. A 12-gon is closer to being a circle than a 6-gon is, so—"
Yuri	"—so the range gets narrower!"
Me	"And if you keep repeating that, you can close in on pi."
Yuri	"How close, though? Is all this going to end with something dumb like 'pi is approximately 3'?"
Me	"Oh ye of little faith. I'm pretty sure that Archimedes was able to get to at least two decimal places, the 3.14 you've been looking for."
Yuri	"Seriously? Then do it! Now!"

4.9 WHY A 96-GON?

Me	"Archimedes repeated this all the way down to using a regular 96-gon."
Yuri	"That's, like, practically a circle!"
Me	"Which is good, because the closer to a circle we get, the better our approximation of pi will be."
Yuri	"Kind of a goofy number to use, though. Why not just crank it up to 100?"
Me	"Because you can't get there by doubling from 6."

$$6 \to 12 \to 24 \to 48 \to 96$$

Yuri   "Ah, doubling. Right. I guess... What's so great about doubling?"

Me   "Because he didn't actually draw 96-gons. He found a way to create $2n$-gons from n-gons."

Yuri   "Explain."

Me   "It works like this. Here's how you create an inscribed 12-gon from an inscribed 6-gon. Do you see the regular 12-gon in there?"

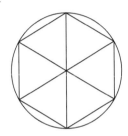 

An inscribed regular 6-gon   An inscribed regular 12-gon

Yuri   "I see it. So?"

Me   "The range gets narrower when you go from 6 to 12, then again from 12 to 24, and so on."

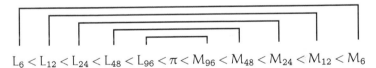

$$L_6 < L_{12} < L_{24} < L_{48} < L_{96} < \pi < M_{96} < M_{48} < M_{24} < M_{12} < M_6$$

Me   "Archimedes kept bumping up the n and calculating L_n and M_n until he got to 96, which he hoped would be really close to pi."

Yuri   "That sounds like a lot of work."

Me　　　　　"Definitely would be if you had to increase n by 1 in every step. That's why he doubled. That's also why he found a way to calculate the new side length when you double the number of sides in an n-gon."

Yuri　　　　"And how did he do that?"

Me　　　　　"It's kinda hard to show using these graphs, so let me draw things a little bigger."

Yuri　　　　"Whatever you need, as long as I get my 3.14."

4.10 Inscribed n-gons to Circumscribed n-gons

Me　　　　　"Let's take a closer look at one side of an inscribed n-gon and a circumscribed n-gon."

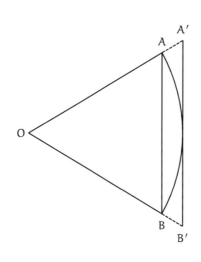

Yuri　　　　"Okay. What am I looking at?"

Me　　　　　"O is the center of a unit circle, AB is one side of an inscribed regular polygon, and A′B′ is one side of a circumscribed regular polygon."

Yuri　　　　"This graph makes me want a slice of pizza."

Me   "A pi pizza instead of a pizza pie?"

            Yuri rolls her eyes.

Yuri   "Just get on with it."

Me   "Okay. What we want is a relation between AB and $A'B'$."

Yuri   "How do we get that?"

Me   "First off, if we can find the length of a side, we'll know the circumference of the n-gon. Because we just have to multiply the side length by n."

Yuri   "Makes sense."

Me   "So let's find that side length. I'm going to name some parts of this graph to make it easier to talk about them."

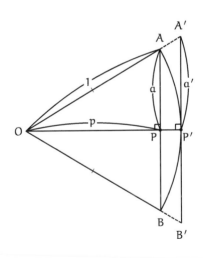

Yuri   "Well that sure complicated things."

Me   "Not too much. Let me make a list of the things I named."

- Point P′ is the point of tangency between line segment A′B′ and the circle.

- Point P is the intersection of segments AB and OP′. Segments AB and OP′ are orthogonal.

Yuri   "Why are we so interested in P and P′?"

Me   "They form these nice triangles, which make it easier to figure out distances."

Yuri   "Okay. Continue."

Me   "On to some line segments."

- Segment OA is the radius of the unit circle, so it has length 1.

- Segment OP has length p.

- Segment AP has length a.

- Segment A′P′ has length a′.

Yuri   "It's all those length labels that's making things such a mess."

Me   "On the contrary. The labels are what'll make our equations nice and tidy."

Yuri   "What equations?"

Me   "Well, for example, what's the length of a side of the inscribed polygon?"

Yuri   "No clue."

Me   "Oh, come on. Look at it, at least."

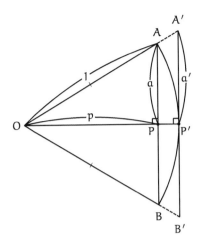

Yuri   "Oh, right. It's just twice a."

Me   "Right. The length of a side equals the length of seg-
        ment AB, and AP and PB have equal lengths, so the
        length of segment AB is $2a$."

Yuri   "Hmm... Triangle $\triangle OAB$ is an isosceles triangle, right?
        Because OA and OB are the same length."

Me   "You're right, but why can you say that those lengths
        are equal?"

Yuri   "Because they're both the radius of the same circle."

Me   "Perfect! Glad to see you're paying attention to the
        graph now."

Yuri   "I have my moments."

Me   "So what I want to do next is use the length of one side
        of an inscribed n-gon, which is $2a$, to find the length of
        one side of a circumscribed n-gon, which is $2a'$. Then
        we'll look at some triangles."

Yuri   "What triangles?"

Me   "$\triangle AOP$ and $\triangle A'OP'$."

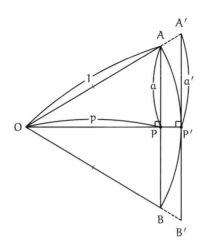

Yuri   "Oh. Okay."

Me   "When you want to think about line segments, it's pretty
              common to use triangles that have those line segments
              as a side. Take a close look at triangles $\triangle AOP$ and
              $\triangle A'OP'$, and tell me what you notice."

Yuri   "They have the same shape."

Me   "Good! The same basic shape, just with different size
              angles, which means they're similar triangles. Specifi-
              cally, they're similar because angles $\angle AOP$ and $\angle A'OP'$
              are the same, and so are angles $\angle APO$ and $\angle A'P'O$."

Yuri   "Okay."

Me   "You've studied how corresponding sides of similar tri-
              angles have the same ratio?"

Yuri   "I have."

Me   "So if we stretch side OP to OP', side AP will extend to
              A'P' in the same proportion. So here's what we get."

$$\overline{OP} : \overline{OP'} = \overline{AP} : \overline{A'P'}$$

$\overline{OP} \to \overline{OP'}$ and $\overline{AP} \to \overline{A'P'}$ extend by the same ratio

$$p : 1 = \overline{AP} : \overline{A'P'} \quad \text{because } \overline{OP} = p \text{ and radius } \overline{OP'} = 1$$

$$p : 1 = a : a' \quad \text{because } \overline{AP} = a \text{ and } \overline{A'P'} = a'$$

$$\frac{p}{1} = \frac{a}{a'} \quad \text{convert ratios to fractions}$$

$$a = pa' \quad \text{multiply both sides by } a' \text{ and swap}$$

Me   "So now you see the relation between a and a'. Right?"

Yuri   "Wait, something's weird here. How can $a = pa'$ when a' is bigger than a?"

Me   "No, that's okay. Because p is less than 1."

Yuri   "Oh, right."

Me   "Actually, maybe instead of $a = pa'$ we should use $a' = \frac{a}{p}$. That gives us a way of going from the side lengths of inscribed polygons to the side lengths of circumscribed ones. Here, let me summarize what we have so far."

Summary 1

Obtaining a circumscribed n-gon from an inscribed n-gon

Let $2a$ be the length of a side of an inscribed regular n-gon, and let $2a'$ be the length of a side of a regular circumscribed n-gon. Then

$$a' = \frac{a}{p},$$

where p is the length of a perpendicular segment drawn from the center of the circle to a side of the inscribed regular n-gon.

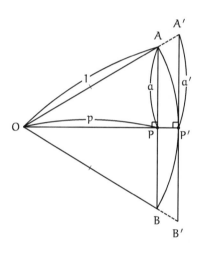

Yuri   "Uh, okay ... Maybe."

Me   "Maybe?"

4.11 Inscribed Regular n-gons

Yuri   "I don't get this p in $a' = \frac{a}{p}$."

Me   "Yeah? That's just the distance from—"

Yuri "Not what I mean. It's that we're trying to find a' from a, so what's this p doing sticking its nose into things? It looks like it's just making a mess of stuff."

Me "Ah, okay. Let's get clear on p, then. Look carefully at the graph."

Yuri "I'm looking."

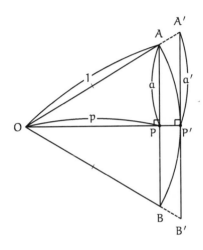

Me "The p is important because we want to use the Pythagorean theorem."

Yuri "How?"

Me "Triangle $\triangle AOP$ is a right triangle, see? So the Pythagorean theorem says that the square of its hypotenuse is the sum of the squares of its sides."

$$\overline{OP}^2 + \overline{AP}^2 = \overline{OA}^2 \qquad \text{Pythagorean theorem for } \triangle AOP$$
$$p^2 + a^2 = 1^2 \qquad \text{because } \overline{OP} = p, \overline{AP} = a, \overline{OA} = 1$$
$$a^2 = 1 - p^2 \qquad \text{move } p^2 \text{ to the right side}$$
$$a = \sqrt{1 - p^2} \qquad a > 0, \text{ so use the positive square root}$$

Yuri	"I understand the Pythagorean theorem, and I can follow how you're moving stuff around, but what are you trying to do? I'm not getting this at all."
Me	"Okay, I guess how to read $a = \sqrt{1 - p^2}$ is something we should look at. There's an a on the left, and a p in the expression on the right. With me so far?"
Yuri	"Yep."
Me	"So you can say that this equation is a way of finding a from p."
Yuri	"Sure, I see that."
Me	"In other words this equation is saying, 'If you can tell me what p is, I can tell you what a is!' "
Yuri	"Wow, it talks and everything."
Me	"Yeah, it's telling us that p is a very important number. If we know p, we know a. And if we know both p and a, then we also know a'."
Yuri	"Huh. We do, don't we."
Me	"Let's write up another summary."

Summary 2

The inscribed regular n-gon

    Let $2a$ be the length of a side of an inscribed regular n-gon, and let p be the length of a perpendicular segment drawn from the center of the circle to a side of the inscribed regular n-gon. Then the following holds:

$$a = \sqrt{1 - p^2}.$$

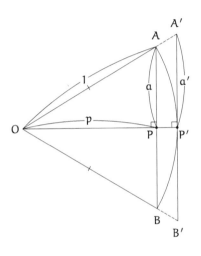

4.12 INSCRIBED n-GONS TO INSCRIBED 2n-GONS

Me   "Okay, let's move on to inscribed regular 2n-gons."

Yuri   "I thought we just did that."

Me   "Be careful. Before, we were talking about inscribed and circumscribed polygons. Now we're talking about two inscribed ones. We want to use an n-gon to find a 2n-gon."

Yuri   "Oh."

Me   "Let's use a new graph. I'm going to get rid of the cir-
            cumscribed polygon, because it would just clutter things
            up."

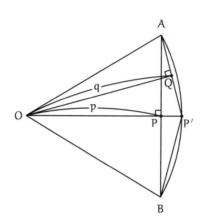

Yuri   "This is the *un*cluttered version?"

Me   "Relatively speaking. But it's not so bad. The only new
            stuff is this line segment AP', and this perpendicular line
            to O."

Yuri   "Why are we interested in AP'?"

Me   "Because that's what's giving us the inscribed $2n$-gon."

Yuri   "Yeah?"

Me   "Do you see where the edges of the n-gon and the $2n$-gon
            are? Look close."

Yuri   "Umm..."

Me   "This long vertical segment AB is a side of the n-gon,
            and these tilted segments AP' and $P'B$ are sides of the
            $2n$-gon. Got it?"

Yuri	"Got it. And this q here is the length of OQ, yeah?"
Me	"Right."
Yuri	"So what are we gonna do with all this?"
Me	"Well what we're aiming for is a formula for converting $\overline{AB}$ into $\overline{AP'}$. We want to use the length of a side of an inscribed regular n-gon to calculate the length of a side of an inscribed regular 2n-gon."
Yuri	"That would be convenient."
Me	"To do it we need to use $\overline{AP} = a$, which is one-half of $\overline{AB}$, to find $\overline{AQ}$, which is one-half of $\overline{AP'}$. And to do *that*, we need to find a way to go from $\overline{OP}$ to $\overline{OQ}$. In other words, we need to represent q in terms of p. That's one way of moving from the n-gon to the 2n-gon, at least."
Yuri	"Wow. Okay."
Me	"Still confusing? Think of the p in an n-gon as being the q in a 2n-gon. If we can find a way of changing p's into q's, we can go all the way from 6 to 12 to 24 to 48 to 96."

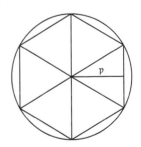

p in a 6 gon

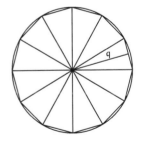

q in a 12-gon

Yuri	"Are we heading towards more equations?"
Me	"Absolutely. An equation that shows the relation between p and q."

Yuri   "And how do we get that?"

Me   "I dunno."

Yuri   "You ... *what?*"

Me   "Still thinking. Gimme a minute."

I spend some time playing with the graph. After
a while I put down my pencil and let out a sigh.

Yuri   "Is it that hard?"

Me   "Well, I know I can force things using trig, but that feels
         like cheating— Hey, wait. I have an idea. Let's add a
         line here ... "

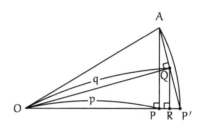

Yuri   "Ugh. You're making it even more complicated!"

Me   "But I think this does the trick. Look, I dropped a per-
         pendicular line from point Q to segment OP′, with its
         foot at R."

Yuri   "Its foot?"

Me   "The point where a perpendicular line intersects some-
         thing is called a perpendicular foot."

Yuri   "If you say so. And?"

Me   "We want to find q from p, so we need to focus on
          this triangle $\triangle QOR$. See how it's similar with trian-
          gle $\triangle AOQ$?"

Yuri   "Again with the similar triangles."

Me   "Sure enough, and just like before we're going to use
          the fact that when you stretch things they stay in pro-
          portion. When you're looking for proportional trian-
          gles, one thing to watch for is their angles—if two trian-
          gles have two equal angles, the triangles are similar. In
          this case angles $\angle AQO$ and $\angle QRO$ are definitely equal,
          since they're both right angles. But can you see how
          angles $\angle AOQ$ and $\angle QOR$ are equal, too?"

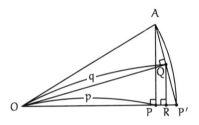

Yuri   "Well, they sure look equal on the graph."

Me   "And they are, but not just because they look that way.
          We know they have to be equal, because segments OA
          and OP' must have equal lengths since they're both
          radii of the same circle. That means triangle $\triangle OP'A$
          is isosceles, so its base angles $\angle OAP'$ and $\angle OP'A$ must
          be equal."

Yuri   "I'm with you so far."

Me   "This means that triangles $\triangle AOQ$ and $\triangle P'OQ$ are con-
          gruent. These two we created by bisecting the isosceles
          triangle, right? So now we know that angles $\angle AOQ$ and

∠P′OQ are equal, and so angles ∠AOQ and ∠QOR must
be equal, too."

Yuri   "Huh."

Me   "In terms of ratios, it looks like this."

$$\overline{OR} : \overline{OQ} = \overline{OQ} : \overline{OA}$$
$$\overline{OR} : q = q : 1 \qquad \text{because } \overline{OQ} = q, \; \overline{OA} = 1$$
$$\overline{OR} = q^2$$

Yuri   "What, you can't make that OR any simpler?"

Me   "Hmm...Well, we know that $\overline{OR} = \overline{OP} + \overline{PR} = p + \overline{PR}$,
            but..."

Yuri   "What's the length of PR?"

Me   "If we can figure that out, we'll have solved the problem."

Yuri   "Well? Can you figure it out?"

Me   "Hang on, I'm thinking."

Yuri   "Hey, is R the midpoint of PP′?"

Me   "Probably, but...Oh, got it!"

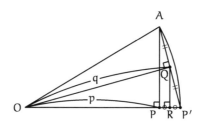

Yuri   "What's this?"

Me   "Triangles $\triangle P'QR$ and $\triangle P'AP$ are similar, with a $2:1$ ratio."

$$
\begin{aligned}
\overline{OR} &= \overline{OP} + \overline{PR} \\
&= p + \overline{PR} & \text{because } \overline{OP} = p \\
&= p + \frac{\overline{PP'}}{2} & \text{because } \overline{PR} = \frac{\overline{PP'}}{2} \\
&= p + \frac{1 - \overline{OP}}{2} & \text{because } \overline{PP'} = \overline{OP'} - \overline{OP} \text{ and } \overline{OP'} = 1 \\
&= p + \frac{1 - p}{2} & \text{because } \overline{OP} = p \\
&= \frac{1 + p}{2}
\end{aligned}
$$

Me   "So now we can use $\overline{OR} = q^2$ and $\overline{OR} = \frac{1+p}{2}$. That means we can say this."

$$
\begin{aligned}
q^2 &= \frac{1 + p}{2} \\
q &= \sqrt{\frac{1 + p}{2}} & \text{because } q > 0
\end{aligned}
$$

Me   "Look! Now we're getting q from p!"

Yuri   "I am so lost."

Me   "Time for summary 3, then."

Summary 3

An inscribed regular n-gon
    Let p be the length of a perpendicular segment drawn from
the center of a circle to a side of an inscribed regular n-gon,
and let q be the length of a perpendicular segment drawn from
the center of the circle to a side of an inscribed regular 2n-gon.
Then the following holds:

$$q = \sqrt{\frac{1+p}{2}}.$$

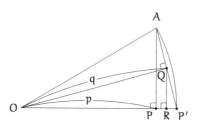

Yuri   "Hate to break it to you dude, but TV is starting to
          sound much more interesting again."

Me   "Hang in there, we're almost done. We've laid down all
          the groundwork to get to the 3.14 you've been wanting
          so badly."

Yuri   "You sure?"

Me   "I am."

4.13 FINALLY REACHING 3.14

Yuri   "I guess I'll trust you, but I'm not catching even a whiff
          of a 3.14 in all that mess."

Me   "Well, the first thing to do is some cleanup, then."

Summaries 1, 2, 3

$$a = \sqrt{1 - p^2} \qquad a \text{ from } p \text{ (p. 159)}$$

$$a' = \frac{a}{p} \qquad a' \text{ from } p, a \text{ (p. 156)}$$

$$q = \sqrt{\frac{1 + p}{2}} \qquad q \text{ from } p \text{ (p. 166)}$$

$$L_n = n \cdot a \qquad L_n \text{ from } a$$

$$M_n = n \cdot a' \qquad M_n \text{ from } a'$$

- $2a$ is the side length of an inscribed regular n-gon.

- $2a'$ is the side length of a circumscribed regular n-gon.

- p is the length of a perpendicular segment drawn from the center of the circle to a side of the inscribed regular n-gon.

- q is the length of a perpendicular segment drawn from the center of the circle to a side of the inscribed regular $2n$-gon.

- $2L_n$ is the perimeter of the inscribed regular n-gon.

- $2M_n$ is the perimeter of the circumscribed regular n-gon.

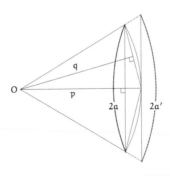

Yuri   "So what do we do now?"

Me   "We take a moment to regret my poor naming of these variables $2a, 2a', p, q$."

Yuri   "Too late for that!"

Me   "Yeah. I should have named these using n's, because when n changes all of these variables will change, too."

Yuri   "Well then why didn't you use n's in the first place?"

Me   "I wanted to keep things simple while thinking through all this stuff. But our next step is to follow in Archimedes' footsteps and increase n through $6 \rightarrow 12 \rightarrow 24 \rightarrow 48 \rightarrow 96$, so from here on out it might be worth putting up with some subscripts. Hang on, let me rewrite this last summary."

Summaries $1, 2, 3$ (with n subscripts)

$$a_n = \sqrt{1 - p_n^2} \qquad\qquad a_n \text{ from } p_n$$

$$a_n' = \frac{a_n}{p_n} \qquad\qquad a_n' \text{ from } p_n, a_n$$

$$p_{2n} = \sqrt{\frac{1 + p_n}{2}} \qquad\qquad p_{2n} \text{ from } p_n$$

$$L_n = n \cdot a_n \qquad\qquad L_n \text{ from } a_n$$

$$M_n = n \cdot a_n' \qquad\qquad M_n \text{ from } a_n'$$

- $2a_n$ is the side length of an inscribed regular n-gon.

- $2a_n'$ is the side length of a circumscribed regular n-gon.

- p_n is the length of a perpendicular segment drawn from the center of the circle to a side of the inscribed regular n-gon.

- p_{2n} is the length of a perpendicular segment drawn from the center of the circle to a side of the inscribed regular $2n$-gon.

- $2L_n$ is the perimeter of the inscribed regular n-gon.

- $2M_n$ is the perimeter of the circumscribed regular n-gon.

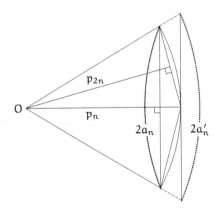

Yuri   "Why'd the q become p_{2n}?"

Me   "Because I was using p for n-gon and q for the 2n-gon."

Yuri   "Okay, whatever. So now what?"

Me   "Well, using this new summary, we can do something like this."

- Get a_n from p_n

- Get a_n' from p_n and a_n

- Get p_{2n} from p_n

Me   "See what I'm doing?"

Yuri   "I think so, yeah."

Me   "We can keep repeating this to find p_6, then p_{12}, then p_{24} and so on. Each p_n will give us a_n and a_n', which will in turn give us L_n and M_n."

Yuri   "Okay."

Me   "Each of those will give us a $2L_n$, which is the perimeter of an inscribed n-gon, and $2M_n$, which is the perimeter of a circumscribed n-gon. Those are going to close in on the value of pi that we're after. The circumference of a circle is $2\pi r$, but since we're using a unit circle $r = 1$, the circumference is just 2π."

$$2L_n < 2\pi < 2M_n$$

Yuri   "So we're getting numbers a little bit smaller and a little bit bigger than pi, like we did before."

Me   "Exactly like that. I gave the perimeters names like $2L_n$ so that we can simplify this inequality a bit, by dividing through by 2."

$$L_n < \pi < M_n$$

Me   "If we're going to begin with a hexagon, here's our start-
              ing point."

$$L_6 < \pi < M_6$$

Yuri   "So L_6 is the perimeter of an inscribed hexagon?"

Me   "Half the perimeter. $2L_6 = 6$, so $L_6 = 3$."

Yuri   "Oh, okay."

Me   "Here, let me draw the regular hexagon. See how
              p_6 is the height of an equilateral triangle with side
              lengths 1? Using the Pythagorean theorem, we get

$$p_6 = \sqrt{1^2 - \left(\frac{1}{2}\right)^2} = \frac{\sqrt{3}}{2}.\text{"}$$

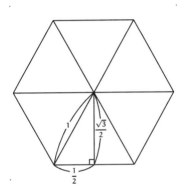

Me   "Now that we know p_6 we can find a_6. Once we know
              p_6 and a_6, we can find a_6'. And when we have a_6', we
              can say that $M_6 = 6 \cdot a_6'$. We just follow the stuff in the
              summary over and over. Please forgive me for using a
              calculator to get the square roots."

$$p_6 = \frac{\sqrt{3}}{2} = 0.866025403$$

$$a_6 = \sqrt{1 - p_6^2} = \sqrt{1 - \left(\frac{\sqrt{3}}{2}\right)^2} = 0.5$$

$$a_6' = \frac{a_6}{p_6} = 0.577350269$$

$$L_6 = 6 \cdot a_6 = 3$$

$$M_6 = 6 \cdot a_6' = 3.464101614$$

Yuri   "What's all this?"

Me   "A calculation of L_6 and M_6. This is the range for pi we get from a hexagon."

Range for pi as determined using regular hexagons

$$3 = L_6 < \pi < M_6 = 3.464101614$$

Pi is some value between 3 and $3.464\cdots$.

Yuri   "3.464? That's not even close! Where's my 3.14!?"

Me   "Don't worry, this is just the first step in our journey, with $n = 6$. Next we do $n = 12$, following along with our last summary."

Yuri   "Fingers crossed."

Me   "Okay, here's the same calculations as before, but with n twice as big."

$$p_{12} = \sqrt{\frac{1 + p_6}{2}} = 0.965925825$$

$$a_{12} = \sqrt{1 - p_{12}^2} = 0.2588190 5$$

$$a_{12}' = \frac{a_{12}}{p_{12}} = 0.267949197$$

$$L_{12} = 12 \cdot a_{12} = 3.1058286$$

$$M_{12} = 12 \cdot a_{12}' = 3.215390364$$

Yuri   "So now we've pinned pi between L_{12} and M_{12}, right? Hey, look at that ..."

Range for pi as determined using regular 12-gons

$$3.1058286 = L_{12} < \pi < M_{12} = 3.215390364$$

Pi is some value between $3.105\cdots$ and $3.215\cdots$.

Me   "Pretty good progress."

Yuri   "Yeah! Keep going!"

Me   "Next is $n = 24$."

$$
\begin{aligned}
p_{24} &= \sqrt{\frac{1 + p_{12}}{2}} &&= 0.99144486 \\
a_{24} &= \sqrt{1 - p_{24}^2} &&= 0.130526204 \\
a'_{24} &= \frac{a_{24}}{p_{24}} &&= 0.131652509 \\
L_{24} &= 24 \cdot a_{24} &&= 3.132628896 \\
M_{24} &= 24 \cdot a'_{24} &&= 3.159660216
\end{aligned}
$$

Range for pi as determined using regular 24-gons

$$3.132628896 = L_{24} < \pi < M_{24} = 3.159660216$$

Pi is some value between $\underline{3.132}\cdots$ and $\underline{3.159}\cdots$.

Yuri   "Whoa! Check it out! A value between 3.13 and 3.15...That's 3.14!"

Me   "Well, not quite. We've verified that pi has to be $3.1\cdots$, but that's not 3.14 yet. The lower limit is $3.132\cdots$, so this leaves the possibility that pi is $3.13\underline{3}\cdots$, for example."

Yuri   "Gah! So picky! Okay, then. Hurry up and do 48!"

Me   "Comin' right up."

$$p_{48} = \sqrt{\frac{1 + p_{24}}{2}} = 0.997858922$$
$$a_{48} = \sqrt{1 - p_{48}^2} = 0.065403149$$
$$a'_{48} = \frac{a_{48}}{p_{48}} = 0.065543482$$
$$L_{48} = 48 \cdot a_{48} = 3.139351152$$
$$M_{48} = 48 \cdot a'_{48} = 3.146087136$$

Yuri   "Hah! There's my 3.14! In M_{48}!"

Me   "Yeah, but L_{48} is still $3.139\cdots$."

Range for pi as determined using regular 48-gons

$$3.139351152 = L_{48} < \pi < M_{48} = 3.146087136$$

Pi is some value between $\underline{3.139}\cdots$ and $\underline{3.146}\cdots$.

Yuri   "So, so close..."

Me   "Looks like we have to go all the way up to 96-gons after all."

Yuri   "Score one for Archimedes."

Me   "Gimme a drumroll?"

Yuri   "Brrr brrr brrr brrr..."

$$p_{96} = \sqrt{\frac{1 + p_{48}}{2}} = 0.999464587$$
$$a_{96} = \sqrt{1 - p_{96}^2} = 0.032719107$$
$$a'_{96} = \frac{a_{96}}{p_{96}} = 0.032736634$$
$$L_{96} = 96 \cdot a_{96} = 3.141034272$$
$$M_{96} = 96 \cdot a'_{96} = 3.142716864$$

Me   "Gotcha!"

Yuri   "3.14 at last!"

Range for pi as determined using regular 96-gons

$$3.14\,1034272 = L_{96} < \pi < M_{96} = 3.1427\,16864$$

Pi is some value between $\underline{3.141}\cdots$ and $\underline{3.142}\cdots$.

Me   "Yep. We can now say with confidence that the value
            of pi is somewhere between $\underline{3.141}\cdots$ and $\underline{3.142}\cdots$. In
            other words—"

Yuri   "In other words, pi is 3.14-something-something-
            something!"

Me   "That's right. We've verified pi to two decimal places."

Yuri   "What a relief."

Closing in on pi using n-gons

n	L_n	$<$	π	$<$	M_n
6	$3.000\cdots$	$<$	π	$<$	$3.464\cdots$
12	$3.105\cdots$	$<$	π	$<$	$3.215\cdots$
24	$3.132\cdots$	$<$	π	$<$	$3.159\cdots$
48	$3.139\cdots$	$<$	π	$<$	$3.146\cdots$
96	$3.141\cdots$	$<$	π	$<$	$3.142\cdots$

Note: Square roots in this dialogue were solved using a calculator. Clearly Archimedes did not have this luxury; he probably evaluated the square roots using something similar to continued fractions. Note that when using a calculator, the final digit in a long number like 3.141034272 or 3.142716864 can be inaccurate.

Credit: Kenji Ueno's *All About Pi* (1999, Nippon Hyoron Sha) was a significant reference for this chapter.

"When *you* see something for the first time, it's an even bigger deal."

Problems for Chapter 4

Problem 4-1 (Measuring pi)

Think of a way to estimate pi using a ruler. For example, measure the circumference and diameter of some cicular object. Call the circumference ℓ and the diameter a. How can you use this information to estimate pi?

(Answer on page 240)

Problem 4-2 (Weighing pi)

Think of a way to estimate pi using a scale. For example, cut a circle of radius a out of heavy construction paper, and weigh it using a precise digital kitchen scale. Next, cut out a square with side length a, and weigh that. Let the weight of the circle be x grams, and that of the square be y grams. How can you use this information to estimate pi?

(Answer on page 240)

Addition Formulas

"Are things that you can see forms?"

5.1 IN THE LIBRARY

One day in the library, doing some after-school math as usual, Tetra joined me at my table.

Tetra   "Hey! Okay if I ask you a question?"

Me   "Sure. What's on your mind?"

Tetra   "Remember the other day, when you taught me about rotating points and trig functions and all?"

Me   "Yeah, sure."

Tetra opens her math notebook.

Tetra   "Well that was really cool, but it's still kinda hard. I've been trying to figure it all out by studying trig some more, but..."

Me   "Impressive. Most people would have given up."

Tetra   "Not me! If I don't do everything I can to keep up with
             stuff, it feels like I'll drown in everything I don't know!"

Me   "So you have a trigonometry question?"

Tetra   "I do! I'm trying to get through the trig section in this
             textbook, but there's so many formulas. I don't know
             how I'm ever going to remember all of these..."

Me   "You're right, there *are* a lot of formulas."

Tetra   "You can say that again! I've been trying to make
             friends with them, but there's just too many to keep
             straight. And the diagrams they use to explain the
             formulas...they're so complicated they make my head
             spin."

Me   "I feel for you. But don't try to take it all in at once.
             You should practice with them one at a time until you
             get used to them. Is there one in particular that's giving
             you problems?"

Tetra   "Hmm, let's see...There were some called the trigono-
             metric addition formulas, I think. Hang on, let me get
             my notebook."

Me   "No need, I know exactly the ones you're thinking of."

5.2 THE ADDITION FORMULA

Me   "I'm pretty sure I can explain them, too. Like for sine
             it's something like this, right?"

Addition formula for $\sin(\alpha + \beta)$

$$\sin(\alpha + \beta) = \sin\alpha\cos\beta + \cos\alpha\sin\beta$$

Tetra   "Whoa, how'd you do that?"

Me	"I've written it so many times I just memorized it. There's lots of memory tricks you can pull, too. I used to think sine–cosine–cosine–sine when I was learning it."
Tetra	"Huh?"
Me	"From the right side of the equation, $\sin \alpha \cos \beta + \cos \alpha \sin \beta$. The alphas and betas always come in the same order, so you just have to remember the order of the functions. Sine and cosine, then cosine and sine."
Tetra	"Oh, okay."
Me	"No need to use that, though. Feel free to make up your own mnemonic."
Tetra	"Hmm, I'll think about it."
Me	"Of course, best of all is to think through this stuff yourself, not just memorize it."
Tetra	"What do you mean?"
Me	"That if you don't understand what the formula *means*, you can't really use it. You need to learn to recognize opportunities to apply the formula when you're doing actual problems."
Tetra	"That makes sense. But what this formula *means*... Hmm..."
Me	"Oh, but don't think that there's only *one* meaning. How you interpret this will change with the problem. You can play around with the equation and discover all kinds of different meanings. It's plenty fun."
Tetra	"I'm so jealous. I'm still at the point where I struggle to discover even one meaning..."
Me	"Well, let's start with just reading it straight off."

$$\sin(\alpha + \beta) = \sin \alpha \cos \beta + \cos \alpha \sin \beta$$

Me   "On the left here, see how we're dealing with a sum of two angles?"

$$\sin(\underbrace{\alpha + \beta}_{\text{sum}}) = \cdots$$

Tetra   "Sure, I see that."

Me   "That's where these formulas get their name—the addition formula. The stuff on the right doesn't have any added angles. Every α and β appears on its own."

$$\cdots = \sin\underbrace{\alpha}\cdot\cos\underbrace{\beta} + \cos\underbrace{\alpha}\cdot\sin\underbrace{\beta}$$

Tetra   "Hey, yeah! Now that you mention it, that's kinda neat."

Me   "Let's say you were working on a problem where it was hard to find $\sin\theta$. Something like this."

- θ is the sum of α and β: $\theta = \alpha + \beta$

- Finding each of $\cos\alpha, \cos\beta, \sin\alpha, \sin\beta$ is easy.

Me   "If you find yourself in a situation like this, the addition formula can be a big help."

Tetra   "I see! So that's how you use this thing."

Me   "One way, at least. Don't forget, there will be others."

Tetra   "Right... Then again, come to think of it that's a lot of conditions. Do situations like that really come up?"

Me   "Well, take the double angle formula $\sin 2\theta = 2\cos\theta\sin\theta$, for example. If you think of 2θ as being $\theta + \theta$ you can use the addition formula. I seem to remember it coming up in calculus, too, when you want to figure out how to differentiate $\sin x$. I think that involved applying the addition formula to $\sin(x + h)$."

Tetra   "Right, right."

Tetra is scribbling in her notebook.

Me
"Was there something about the addition formula that was giving you problems?"

Tetra
"Not so much the formula itself as the graph my book used to explain it. What a mess! I couldn't make heads or tails of it."

Me
"Well then, how about we create that graph, figuring things out as we go along. If we do it together I'm sure you'll get it. It should also make the formula itself a lot clearer."

Tetra
"Well I'm all for that!"

5.3 STARTING WITH THE UNIT CIRCLE

Me
"Okay, so what we're after is finding out how the trigonometric addition formula works. In other words, why $\sin(\alpha + \beta) = \sin \alpha \cos \beta + \cos \alpha \sin \beta$."

Tetra
"Right!"

Me
"One condition, though. If we want to do it for all angles, we have to break things down into cases, so for now we're going to assume that α and β are both angles greater than $0°$, and that $\alpha + \beta$ is less than $90°$."

Tetra
"Gotcha."

Me
"Let's warm up by drawing a unit circle, a circle with radius 1, and finding the relation between the sine and cosine functions."

Tetra
"Okay."

Me
"Letting the origin be our center of rotation, we start by rotating a point $(1, 0)$ by angle α along the circumference of the circle. Here's what that looks like as a graph."

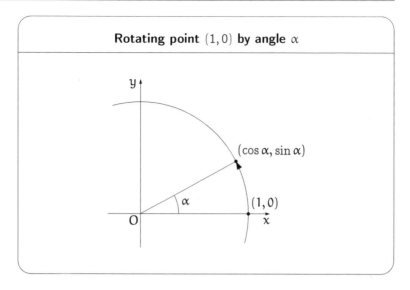

Rotating point $(1,0)$ by angle α

Tetra   "I remember this! The x-coordinate is $\cos\alpha$, and the y-coordinate is $\sin\alpha$."

Me   "Right. You can even think of this as being the definition of the sine function. Okay, your turn. Try rotating the point by some other angle β."

Tetra   "Like this?"

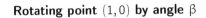

Rotating point $(1, 0)$ **by angle** β

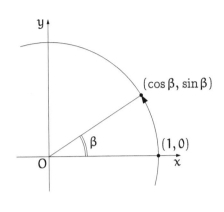

Me   "My bad, I didn't explain that right. You just rotated point $(1, 0)$ by angle β, right?"

Tetra   "I tried to, at least. Did I do it wrong?"

Me   "No, no. Your graph is right. But what I had in mind what something like this."

Rotating point $(\cos\alpha, \sin\alpha)$ **by angle** β

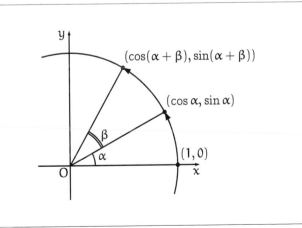

Tetra   "Oh, you added another rotation to the first one!"

Me   "Exactly! When we rotate a point $(1, 0)$ by angle α we
               end up at point $(\cos \alpha, \sin \alpha)$, right? So when we rotate
               that point a little more, by an additional angle β, we end
               up at point $(\cos(\alpha + \beta), \sin(\alpha + \beta))$. The progression is
               like this."

$$(1, 0) \quad \overset{\alpha}{\to} \quad (\cos \alpha, \sin \alpha) \quad \overset{\beta}{\to} \quad (\cos(\alpha + \beta), \sin(\alpha + \beta))$$

Tetra   "Oh, I get it! Rotating by angle α and then again by an-
               gle β is the same as adding them up from the beginning
               and *swooop,* rotating by angle $\alpha + \beta$ all at once."

Me   "A perfect description."

$$(1, 0) \quad \overset{\alpha + \beta}{\longrightarrow} \quad (\cos(\alpha + \beta), \sin(\alpha + \beta))$$

Tetra   "I've got that, then. What's next?"

Me   "Well, look at this. We wanted to find $\sin(\alpha + \beta)$, and
               after rotating the point its y-coordinate should be sitting
               right on $\sin(\alpha + \beta)$!"

After rotating a point $(1,0)$ by $\alpha + \beta$, its y-coordinate is
$\sin(\alpha + \beta)$.

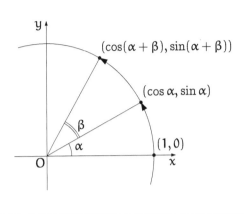

Tetra   "Oh, right. We're doing the addition formula, which is all about $\alpha + \beta$. So where does this take us?"

Me   "Well, we've found the $\sin(\alpha + \beta)$ part of the addition formula, so now let's look for the $\sin \alpha \cos \beta + \cos \alpha \sin \beta$ part. While we're at it, we'd like to see how those are the same, like the formula tells us."

Our search for $\sin(\alpha + \beta) = \sin \alpha \cos \beta + \cos \alpha \sin \beta$

- We've found $\sin(\alpha + \beta)$, the left side of this trignonometric addition formula.

- We want to find $\sin \alpha \cos \beta + \cos \alpha \sin \beta$, the right side of the formula.

- We also want to confirm that the two sides are equal.

Tetra   "I see! We're looking at this problem by taking it to the world of graphs!"

Me   "Right!"

Tetra   "But still...It's all so complex. I'm not sure I can find
            it, even in a graph..."

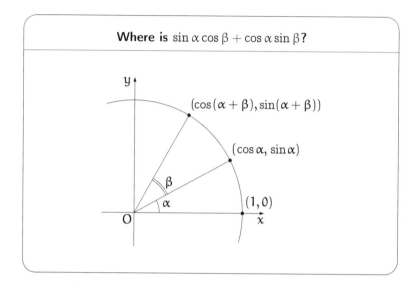

Where is $\sin\alpha\cos\beta + \cos\alpha\sin\beta$?

5.4 SOLVING PART OF THE PROBLEM

Me   "Do you remember the other day, when Miruka was talk-
            ing about Pólya's *How to Solve It*?"

Tetra   "Sure. He was the one with all those questions, right?"

Me   "Yep, questions to ask yourself when you're working on
            a problem, but aren't sure what to do. One of those
            questions was, 'Can I solve part of the problem?'"

A question from Pólya

Can I solve part of the problem?

Tetra   "Well that's fine and all, but what would be part of
            $\sin \alpha \cos \beta + \cos \alpha \sin \beta$?"

Me   "How about this $\sin \beta$ at the end here?"

$$\sin \alpha \cos \beta + \cos \alpha \underbrace{\sin \beta}_{\uparrow}$$

Tetra   "Just the $\sin \beta$? Like this?"

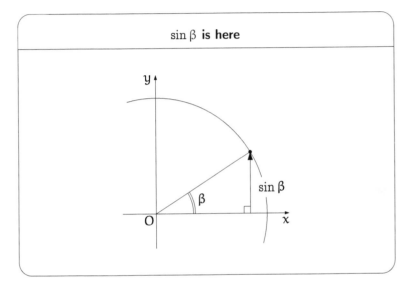

sin β **is here**

Me   "Well, yeah, but we want to find it in the graph of $\sin(\alpha +$
            $\beta)$. See how it's also here, in this triangle?"

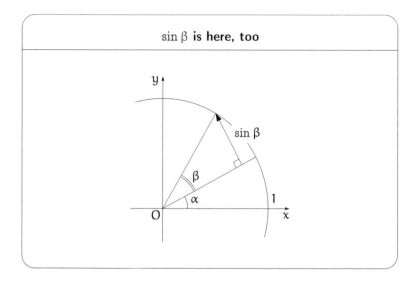

sin β **is here, too**

Tetra   "But isn't that the triangle I just drew, rotated by α?"

Me   "Hm? Yeah, it is, isn't it."

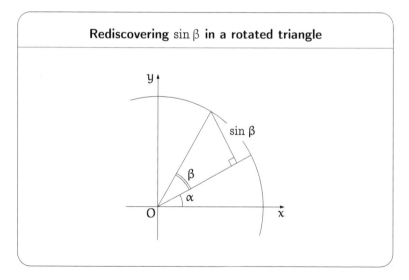

Rediscovering sin β **in a rotated triangle**

Me   "Anyway, congratulations. You've found part of the expression we're investigating."

Tetra   "Nailed ya', sin β!"

$$\sin \alpha \cos \beta + \cos \alpha \underbrace{\sin \beta}_{\text{found it!}}$$

Me   "So let's look for another part. How about the cos β?"

Tetra   "No problem, I've already found it. Here, right?"

Me   "You're catching on fast!"

Tetra   "Well I drew the triangle, after all."

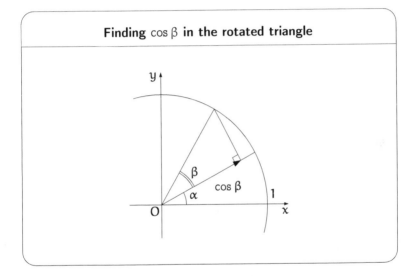

Finding cos β in the rotated triangle

Me   "Okay, add cos β to the list of our discoveries."

$$\sin \alpha \underbrace{\cos \beta}_{\text{found it!}} + \cos \alpha \underbrace{\sin \beta}_{\text{found it!}}$$

Tetra   "Yeah, but ..."

Me   "But what?"

Tetra   "We've still got to multiply those by sin α and cos α."

Me   "We do indeed. Let's look at the graph and think care-
              fully about what that means."

              Tetra's face clouds over.

Me   "What's wrong?"

Tetra   "It's just that... Well, this is probably kind of dumb,
              but even though I think I'm following everything you
              say, when there's all these letters and stuff it all gets so
              confusing. It's hard to think carefully, because I have no
              idea what I should be thinking about!"

Me   "That's not dumb at all. It happens to everyone when
              you're doing something new. When it does, try to run
              through more of Pólya's questions."

Tetra   "Like what?"

Me   "Well, a good one to always keep in mind is, 'What are
              you trying to find?'"

A question from Pólya

What am I trying to find?

Tetra   "I guess we're trying to find $\sin \alpha \cos \beta + \cos \alpha \sin \beta$."

Me   "We are. And to find that, we need to understand what
              $\sin \alpha \cos \beta$ and $\cos \alpha \sin \beta$ are."

Tetra   "The two things we're adding, right."

Me   "Another Pólya question, then."

A question from Pólya

What information have I been given?

Tetra   "Umm... We've been given α and β."

Me   "And using those we've found $\cos \beta$ and $\sin \beta$. We know part of their relation to the bigger problem, too."

$$\sin \alpha \underbrace{\cos \beta}_{\text{this and...}} + \cos \alpha \underbrace{\sin \beta}_{\text{this}}$$

Tetra   "Right."

Me   "So let's think like this: is it possible to create what we're after, from what we have? In other words, can we create $\sin \alpha \cos \beta$ and $\cos \alpha \sin \beta$ from $\cos \beta$ and $\sin \beta$?"

Tetra's eyes widen and gleam.

Tetra   "Okay, let me think about this, see if we can't use that to move ahead."

Can we create $\sin \alpha \cos \beta$ from $\cos \beta$ and $\sin \beta$?

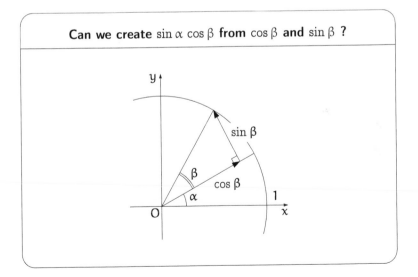

After some fiddling with the graph, Tetra looks
up with a grin.

Tetra   "I found something! We can get $\sin \alpha \cos \beta$ here, from
             $\triangle AOH$!"

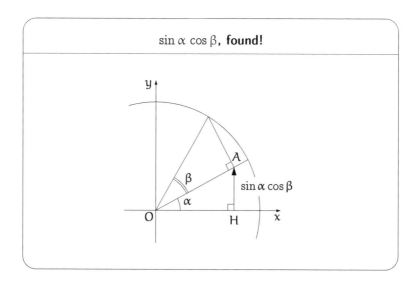

$\sin \alpha \cos \beta$, **found!**

In the right triangle $\triangle AOH$, from the definition of $\sin \alpha$

$$\sin \alpha = \frac{\overline{HA}}{\overline{OA}}.$$

In other words,

$$\overline{HA} = \overline{OA} \sin \alpha.$$

From this, we have

$$
\begin{aligned}
\overline{HA} &= \overline{OA} \sin \alpha \\
&= \cos \beta \sin \alpha \qquad \text{because } \overline{OA} = \cos \beta \\
&= \sin \alpha \cos \beta. \qquad \text{changed the order of multiplication}
\end{aligned}
$$

Me   "Well done! And now another piece of the puzzle falls
            into place."

$$\underbrace{\sin \alpha \cos \beta}_{\text{this and}\ldots} + \cos \alpha \underbrace{\sin \beta}_{\text{this}}$$

Tetra   "Ooh, that feels good."

Me   "Now all that's left is—"

Tetra   "Finding $\cos \alpha \sin \beta$!"

After Tetra spends a good while looking, I give her a nudge.

Me   "Tetra, it's right here."

Tetra   "Hey, no spoilers!"

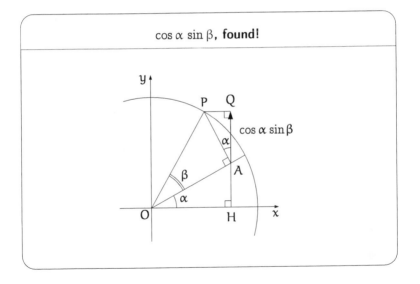

$\cos \alpha \sin \beta$, **found!**

The sum of the interior angles of a triangle is 180°, so the measure α of $\angle AOH$ in the right triangle $\triangle AOH$ must be 180° less $\angle OAH$ less the right angle $\angle AHO$. In other words,

$$\alpha = 180° - \angle OAH - 90°.$$

Similarly, the measure of $\angle PAQ$ is $\angle HAQ$, which is 180° less $\angle OAH$ less the right angle $\angle OAP$. In other words,

$$\angle PAQ = 180° - \angle OAH - 90°.$$

From the above, we have that

$$\angle PAQ = \alpha.$$

Now considering the right triangle $\triangle PAQ$, from the definition of $\cos \alpha$ we have

$$\cos \alpha = \frac{\overline{AQ}}{\overline{PA}}.$$

In other words,

$$\overline{AQ} = \overline{PA} \cos \alpha.$$

Therefore, we can say that

$$
\begin{aligned}
\overline{AQ} &= \overline{PA} \cos \alpha && \text{from the definition of } \cos \alpha \\
&= \sin \beta \cos \alpha && \text{because } \overline{PA} = \sin \beta \\
&= \cos \alpha \sin \beta && \text{change order of multiplication}
\end{aligned}
$$

Me   "Oops, sorry."

Tetra   "No, I shouldn't have yelled. Anyway, we found all the parts now, right?"

$$\underbrace{\sin \alpha \cos \beta} + \underbrace{\cos \alpha \sin \beta}$$

Me   "We have! And that's all we needed to see from the graph that $\sin(\alpha + \beta)$ and $\sin \alpha \cos \beta + \cos \alpha \sin \beta$ are indeed equivalent!"

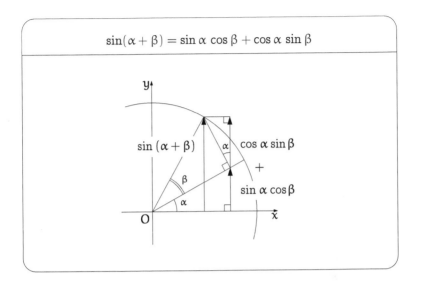

$$\sin(\alpha + \beta) = \sin \alpha \cos \beta + \cos \alpha \sin \beta$$

Tetra   "Yay!"

5.5 LOOKING BACK

Tetra   "I've noticed something..."

Me   "What's that?"

Tetra   "Before I was whining about the graphs in my textbook, right?"

Me   "I wouldn't go so far as calling it whining, but whatever."

Tetra   "Anyway, I think my problem is that I was just *looking* at the graphs, not actually doing stuff myself. All this makes so much more sense when I see it drawn out, as we work through stuff."

Me   "So what's the lesson to be learned?"

Tetra	"That when a diagram looks too complex to figure out, I need to simplify things, and rewrite it myself."
Me	"Same with equations, too. There's a lot to be learned by putting pencil to paper."
Tetra	"I think I've also been thinking about things all wrong."
Me	"How so?"
Tetra	"I'm too...unfocused. I need to start using these questions from Pólya."

Some questions from Pólya

- Can I solve part of the problem?

- What am I looking for?

- What information have I been given?

Me	"I think that would be a big help. I use them myself whenever I'm working on a tough problem."
Tetra	"I've never consciously asked myself questions like this. I need to pick up some of your good habits. I guess that's what I'm looking for right now."
Me	"Anyway, that was fun. You're a good listener, so I'm always happy to help with this kind of stuff."
Tetra	"Thanks!"
Me	"Hey, I just remembered another good Pólya question, one for when you look back at what you've done: can you see it at a glance?"

Tetra   "At...a glance?"

Me   "Sure. We've convinced ourselves that this $\sin(\alpha + \beta) =$ $\cdots$ formula works, but have we made that obvious?"

Tetra   "Um..."

Me   "Let's look at the diagram like this. It should make it easier to see the flow from 1."

$$1 \to \cos\beta \to \sin\alpha\cos\beta$$

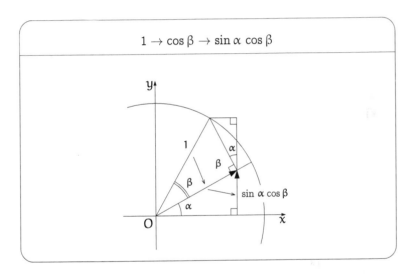

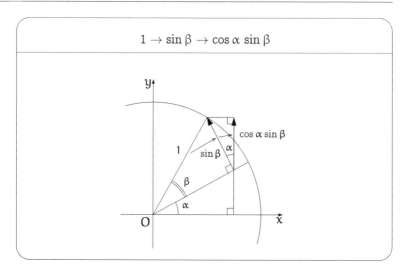

$$1 \to \sin \beta \to \cos \alpha \sin \beta$$

Tetra   "I see! I'll do this all again on my own, later."

Me   "Good. The trigonometric addition formula looks complex at first, but once you've drawn these graphs on your own it's not so hard to remember."

Trigonometric addition formula

$$\sin(\alpha + \beta) = \sin \alpha \cos \beta + \cos \alpha \sin \beta$$

Tetra   "Actually, I think I've already got sine–cosine–cosine–sine stuck in my head."

Me   "Welcome to the club!"

Tetra   "Y'know, it's funny how these rotating points showed up again. I guess they're more important than I expected at first."

Me   "Well, we did use them to define the sine and cosine functions, so it's no surprise that they show up all over the place."

Tetra   "I guess you're right. Before I'd only associated trigonometry with triangles, but now I see how important it is to think about the circles that are creating those triangles."

Me   "Exactly. Once you get used to looking at it that way, it becomes hard to separate the circles and the triangles."

Trigonometry is about both triangles and circles

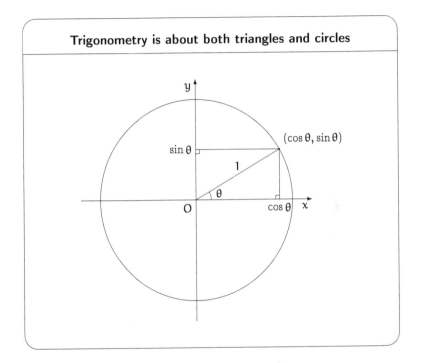

5.6 DESCRIBING ROTATIONS

Me   "Now that you mention it, we never finished our talk about rotating points."

Tetra   "Yeah, I think we just ended with some really complicated equations."

Me   "We were using something like this, I think. Rotating a point (a, b) around the origin by some angle θ to a new point (a', b'), right?"

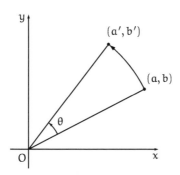

Tetra   "That's the one."

Me   "And we said you could calculate the new coordinates
               like this."

Rotation equations (see p. 120)

- Let the origin $(0, 0)$ be the center of rotation.

- Call the angle of rotation θ.

- Call the point to rotate (a, b).

- Call the point after rotation (a', b').

Given the above, we can use a, b, and θ to represent a' and b'
as follows:
$$\begin{cases} a' & = a \cos \theta - b \sin \theta \\ b' & = a \sin \theta + b \cos \theta \end{cases}$$

Tetra   "Sure, I remember this! But, wow, how are you able to
               just write all that stuff down off the top of your head?
               Did you memorize all that?"

Me   "It's not really memorization. Just remember the graph
               Miruka drew for us, and it's not too hard to duplicate
               everything from that."

Tetra   "What diagram?"

Me   "The one with the rotated rectangle, remember?"

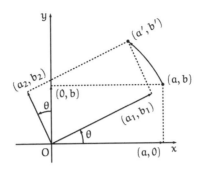

Tetra   "Oh, right! We added up the respective coordinates, right?"

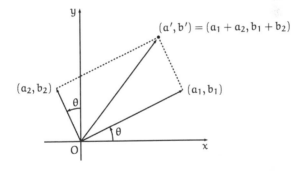

Me   "Yep. And we found that all you need to know is $\cos\theta$ and $\sin\theta$."

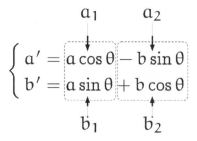

Tetra	"Gee, I should have remembered all this. We just did it a few days ago..."
Me	"It's a lot to take in."
Tetra	"Such a complicated solution though."
Me	"Yeah, it is a bit complex, I guess."
Miruka	"Just a bit."
Me	"Whoa!"
Tetra	"Hi, Miruka!"

5.7 MATRICES

Miruka	"Let's continue the conversation then, and talk about rotation matrices. That should make things easier. How are you with matrices, Tetra?"
Tetra	"Er... I've heard of them, but I have no idea what they are."
Me	"I'll give you a quick rundown, then."
Tetra	"Please do!"
Me	"Matrices are used in advanced math all the time, but don't worry—it's a simple concept. You usually write them as a table of numbers surrounded by big parentheses, like this."

$$\begin{pmatrix} 1 & 2 \\ 3 & 4 \end{pmatrix}$$

Tetra	"Okay."
Me	"The numbers here are called elements of the matrix. Elements don't have to be numbers, though. They can be letter variables, or mathematical expressions, or whatever. Here's a matrix with variables as elements."

$$\begin{pmatrix} a & b \\ c & d \end{pmatrix}$$

Tetra	"Question!"
Me	"Ask away."
Tetra	"How am I supposed to read that? Is it a–b–c–d, or a–c–b–d?"
Me	"Ah, good question. The answer depends on if you want to read off rows or columns. You can do it either way, just like with a table."

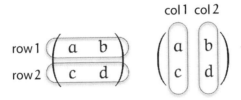

Tetra	"Oh, I see. There's both rows of two elements, and columns of two elements. Neat!"
Miruka	"Don't get hung up on the 'two elements' thing, though. That's just for his example here. A matrix can have as many rows and columns as you need."
Tetra	"Got it!"

Me   "Oh, and if you want to add or multiply matrices you
            just—"

Miruka   "That's enough."

            Miruka holds up a hand.

Miruka   "Let's just jump straight to rotation matrices."

Me   "Yeah?"

Tetra   "Really?"

Miruka   "The fundamentals of matrices are important, granted,
            but I want to get to the fun stuff."

Tetra   "Are you sure I'll be able to follow along?"

Miruka   "Positive. We'll be simplifying the complex. I think
            you'll like it."

Tetra   "Well then, lead the way!"

5.8 THE ROTATION EQUATION

Miruka   "So here's the formulas for rotation that you found to be
            too complex."

$$\begin{cases} a' & = a\cos\theta - b\sin\theta \\ b' & = a\sin\theta + b\cos\theta \end{cases}$$

Rotation formulas

Tetra   "Well, sure. I mean, look at them!"

Miruka   "When I look at them, I see a sum of products."

Tetra   "A ... what?"

Me   "Oh, sure! Multiply–multiply–add!"

Miruka   "Cute. You should set that to music."

Me   "Only if you'll dance to it."

Miruka   "Anyway, both of the formulas have this multiply–multiply–add pattern."

$$a' = a\cos\theta - b\sin\theta = \underbrace{\underbrace{\text{ⓐ} \times \boxed{\cos\theta}}_{\text{multiply}} + \underbrace{\text{ⓑ} \times \boxed{-\sin\theta}}_{\text{multiply}}}_{\text{add}}$$

$$b' = a\sin\theta + b\cos\theta = \underbrace{\underbrace{\text{ⓐ} \times \boxed{\sin\theta}}_{\text{multiply}} + \underbrace{\text{ⓑ} \times \boxed{\cos\theta}}_{\text{multiply}}}_{\text{add}}$$

Tetra   "Multiply–multiply–add! Multiply–multiply–add! I like it!"

Miruka   "Let's make a matrix out of the stuff in boxes here."

$$\begin{pmatrix} \boxed{\cos\theta} & \boxed{-\sin\theta} \\ \boxed{\sin\theta} & \boxed{\cos\theta} \end{pmatrix}$$

A matrix

Tetra   "What's the—"

Miruka   "There's only two things in circles, an ⓐ and a ⓑ. Let's stack them up and make a vector."

$$\begin{pmatrix} \text{ⓐ} \\ \text{ⓑ} \end{pmatrix}$$

A vector

Tetra	"But what—"

Miruka	"Now we pair the two, and call this the product of a matrix and a vector."

$$\left(\boxed{\cos\theta} \quad \boxed{-\sin\theta} \right) \left(\boxed{a} \atop \boxed{b} \right)$$

The product of a matrix and a vector

Tetra	"I don't—"

Miruka	"We'll use your multiply–multiply–add to define the product like this."

$$\left(\boxed{\cos\theta} \atop \boxed{\sin\theta} \quad \boxed{-\sin\theta} \atop \boxed{\cos\theta} \right) \left(\boxed{a} \atop \boxed{b} \right) = \left(\boxed{a} \times \boxed{\cos\theta} + \boxed{b} \times \boxed{-\sin\theta} \atop \boxed{a} \times \boxed{\sin\theta} + \boxed{b} \times \boxed{\cos\theta} \right)$$

Defining the product of a matrix and a vector

Tetra	"Hold up! I can't take anymore, I'll explode! Gimme some time to figure out what's being multiplied by what."

Miruka	"Take as much as you need."

Tetra begins taking notes, looking back and forth between her notebook and Miruka's equation. I notice she's writing the same equation several times.

Tetra	"It looks like you're doing these two calculations. Is that right?"

$$\left(\boxed{\cos\theta}\;\;\boxed{-\sin\theta}\right)\begin{pmatrix}\text{\textcircled{a}}\\\text{\textcircled{b}}\end{pmatrix} = \left(\text{\textcircled{a}}\times\boxed{\cos\theta}+\text{\textcircled{b}}\times\boxed{-\sin\theta}\right)$$

$$\left(\boxed{\sin\theta}\;\;\boxed{\cos\theta}\right)\begin{pmatrix}\text{\textcircled{a}}\\\text{\textcircled{b}}\end{pmatrix} = \left(\text{\textcircled{a}}\times\boxed{\sin\theta}+\text{\textcircled{b}}\times\boxed{\cos\theta}\right)$$

Miruka   "You've got it."

Tetra   "And you called this a product?"

Miruka   "Yes. We've represented the rotation formulas as the product of a matrix and a vector."

Vector   Array   Vector

$$\begin{pmatrix}a'\\b'\end{pmatrix} = \begin{pmatrix}\cos\theta & -\sin\theta\\\sin\theta & \cos\theta\end{pmatrix}\begin{pmatrix}a\\b\end{pmatrix}$$

Point after rotation   Rotation matrix   Point before rotation

Tetra   "But...a *product*? Like in multiplication? I'm afraid I still don't get this."

Miruka   "What don't you get?"

Tetra   "I'm sorry, I—"

Miruka   "Stop apologizing. *What don't you get?*"

Tetra   "I— Okay. I understand that this is called a matrix. We're lining the numbers up a certain way, and we're calling that a matrix, right?"

$$\begin{pmatrix}\cos\theta & -\sin\theta\\\sin\theta & \cos\theta\end{pmatrix}$$

Miruka   "Right. Go on."

Tetra   "I also understand that this is called a vector. We're putting the a-coordinate of point (a, b) above the b-coordinate, and calling that a vector, yeah?"

$$\begin{pmatrix} a \\ b \end{pmatrix}$$

Miruka	"Still good. A vertical one like that is called a column vector. What else?"
Tetra	"Okay, so that's what I understand—vectors and matrices. I understand that those are names we've assigned to these things, at least. But when you line them up in an expression like that . . ."

$$\begin{pmatrix} \cos\theta & -\sin\theta \\ \sin\theta & \cos\theta \end{pmatrix} \begin{pmatrix} a \\ b \end{pmatrix}$$

Tetra	"I don't understand how just putting them next to each other is somehow multiplication. How you can use this in an equation."
Me	"That's why I say we should stick with the basics of—"
Miruka	"No. She can do this. She can read about the basics in a book on her own time. But that's not what she wants to know now, and it isn't a lack of information that's confusing her."
Tetra	"I, uh—"

Miruka points a finger at Tetra.

| Miruka | "Tetra, explain to me once more what you're confused about." |
| Tetra | "Um, okay. So, you said we can represent the rotation formulas as a product of a matrix and a vector." |

$$\begin{cases} a' &= a\cos\theta - b\sin\theta \\ b' &= a\sin\theta + b\cos\theta \end{cases}$$

The rotation formulas

$$\begin{pmatrix} a' \\ b' \end{pmatrix} = \begin{pmatrix} \cos\theta & -\sin\theta \\ \sin\theta & \cos\theta \end{pmatrix} \begin{pmatrix} a \\ b \end{pmatrix}$$

Written as the product of a matrix and a vector

Miruka   "And?"

Tetra   "Well, the first thing that popped into my head was, *why*? I don't see where this came from—it's like it fell out of the sky!"

Miruka   "Hmph."

Tetra   "I mean, a product is when you're multiplying something, right? I think I understand what a matrix and a vector are, but I don't understand how this is multiplying them. Where does this multiply–multiply–add thing come from? *Why* does this work?"

Tetra looks back and forth between Miruka and me.

Tetra   "When I get a *why* like that, one that I can't answer, it just makes me want to scream. It makes me think that...I don't know, that math is too hard for me or something."

Me   "Tetra, I—"

Tetra   "This happens to me all the time. When it happens in class at least I can ask questions—well, sometimes I can. But when I'm trying to do math alone..."

Miruka   "Is that so."

Tetra   "Oh, yeah, it happens all the time. I get in this funk about how little I know, how little I really understand, and...I lose confidence in myself, and get kinda depressed. It gets to where I can't even hear what my teacher is saying."

Miruka	"What about now?"
Tetra	"Huh?"
Miruka	"Can you hear what I'm saying?"
Tetra	"Uh, yeah. Sure."
Miruka	"Let's get back to the math, then."
Tetra	"Right. Sorry, I had kind of a meltdown there."
Miruka	"Stop apologizing. This defines how we're multiplying the matrix and the vector."

$$\begin{pmatrix} \boxed{\cos\theta} & \boxed{-\sin\theta} \\ \boxed{\sin\theta} & \boxed{\cos\theta} \end{pmatrix} \begin{pmatrix} \textcircled{a} \\ \textcircled{b} \end{pmatrix} = \begin{pmatrix} \textcircled{a} \times \boxed{\cos\theta} + \textcircled{b} \times \boxed{-\sin\theta} \\ \textcircled{a} \times \boxed{\sin\theta} + \textcircled{b} \times \boxed{\cos\theta} \end{pmatrix}$$

Definition of vector–matrix multiplication

Miruka	"This won't cut it for the general case, but it's enough for a rotation matrix and a point vector so this is what we'll use. It's a definition, so it doesn't need any other justification. That also means there's no reason to freak out if you don't understand the *why* of it."
Tetra	"Okay, but—"
Miruka	"You were cool with naming things like matrices and vectors, so you should be just as cool with naming something 'the product of a matrix and a vector.' In this case we're just naming an operation, instead of a thing."
Tetra	"Oh... Oh!"
Miruka	"You're letting words trip you up. The product of two numbers is different from the product of a matrix and a vector. 'Product' can mean different things, depending on what you're trying to find the product of."

Tetra	"So it's like a homonym?"
Miruka	"If you prefer."
Tetra	"Oh. Okay. Wow, that clears things up."
Miruka	"That's why definitions are so important. Not that these definitions were created on a whim. They did it this way because it's useful."
Tetra	"Who did?"
Miruka	"Who did what?"
Tetra	"Who defined the products of matrices and vectors like this?"
Miruka	"A mathematician named Cayley, some time in the mid-nineteenth century."
Me	"Cayley, as in Cayley and Hamilton?"
Miruka	"That's the one."
Tetra	"And I suppose he had a good reason for defining them like this?"
Miruka	"He did. He was writing a paper on systems of equations, and found it convenient to do things this way. That's reason enough."
Tetra	"Can I assume that since these things have a definition, they're important enough that I should remember them?"
Miruka	"Clever girl. You'll see expressions in this form—the dot product—all the time when you start working with vectors. Also remember that definitions are normally used for things that can't be derived from something else. "
Tetra	"Okay, I'm good with all that so far, but ..."

I was drawn in by Tetra and Miruka's conversation, watching Tetra describe her frustration when faced with something she didn't understand, and Miruka's response. On the surface it was a discussion of mathematics, but on some different level, it was two people sharing their passion.

Tetra   "But I must be missing something. You said using vectors and matrices should make this easier, but I'm not seeing that at *all*. What's easier about all this?"

Miruka   "Hmph. My mistake. I shouldn't have used the E-word. I'll tell you what, let's look at matrices from a slightly different angle—how we can use them to get a new perspective on things."

Tetra   "What kind of perspective?"

Miruka   "Like, how using matrices lets us show revolution itself as a mathematical expression."

5.9 A NEW PERSPECTIVE

Miruka   "Look at how the rotation formulas have $\cos\theta$'s and $\sin\theta$'s scattered all over the place."

$$\begin{cases} a' &= a\cos\theta - b\sin\theta \\ b' &= a\sin\theta + b\cos\theta \end{cases}$$

The rotation formulas

Me   "They do indeed."

Miruka   "But when we represent the rotation formulas as matrices the $\cos\theta$'s and $\sin\theta$'s are all neatly tucked away in the matrix. That makes everything easier to read."

$$\begin{pmatrix} a' \\ b' \end{pmatrix} = \begin{pmatrix} \cos\theta & -\sin\theta \\ \sin\theta & \cos\theta \end{pmatrix} \begin{pmatrix} a \\ b \end{pmatrix}$$

The rotation formulas in matrix/vector form

Tetra   "Hmm, that is a bit neater, isn't it."

Miruka   "When you use matrices like this, everything having to do with the rotation is packed into the rotation matrix. Then all you have to do is whack it with a vector representing the point you want to rotate, and *bang*, there's your rotation. It's like tossing points into a machine that rotates them and spits them back out."

$$\begin{pmatrix} a' \\ b' \end{pmatrix} \longleftarrow \begin{pmatrix} \cos\theta & -\sin\theta \\ \sin\theta & \cos\theta \end{pmatrix} \longleftarrow \begin{pmatrix} a \\ b \end{pmatrix}$$

Toss points at the rotation matrix, and it gives you rotated points.

Tetra   "I love this diagram."

Me   "I'm pretty sure we all saw something similar when we first learned about functions."

Miruka   "Using a rotation matrix lets you clearly show what it is that's rotating things. That's the new perspective I was talking about. Replace it with another matrix that does something else and you can get a completely different transformation. Don't underestimate matrices—they're a marvelous tool for representing things."

Tetra   "But they seem so...hard."

Miruka   "You just need to spend some quality time with them."

Tetra   "I'll try...By the way, where does this multiply–multiply–add pattern come from?"

Miruka   "Answer me this, first. With the origin as the center of rotation, if you rotate a point $(1, 0)$ by an angle α, where does it end up?"

Tetra   "Oh, I know this one now. At $(\cos\alpha, \sin\alpha)$! The x-coordinate is the cosine and the y-coordinate is the sine!"

Miruka   "Good. Another question: with the origin still as the center of rotation, if you rotate a point $(\cos\alpha, \sin\alpha)$ by an angle β, where does that one end up?"

Tetra   "Well, we just did that using the definition of matrix and vector products, so isn't it this?"

$$\begin{pmatrix} \cos\beta & -\sin\beta \\ \sin\beta & \cos\beta \end{pmatrix} \begin{pmatrix} \cos\alpha \\ \sin\alpha \end{pmatrix} = \begin{pmatrix} \cos\alpha\cos\beta - \sin\alpha\sin\beta \\ \cos\alpha\sin\beta + \sin\alpha\cos\beta \end{pmatrix}$$

Miruka   "What's the y-coordinate after the revolution?"

Tetra   "Um, this mess."

$$\cos\alpha\sin\beta + \sin\alpha\cos\beta$$

Miruka   "That's all?"

Tetra   "Isn't it?"

Miruka   "Try swapping the order of addition."

$$\sin\alpha\cos\beta + \cos\alpha\sin\beta$$

Tetra   "Oh! Sine–cosine–cosine–sine! That's the addition formula!"

Miruka   "Right. The multiply–multiply–add pattern is hidden in there, too."

$$\sin(\alpha + \beta) = \underbrace{\sin\alpha\cos\beta}_{\text{multiply}} + \underbrace{\cos\alpha\sin\beta}_{\text{multiply}}$$
$$\underbrace{}_{\text{add}}$$

Me   "Well whaddaya know..."

Miruka "Here's a summary of the addition formulas for sine and cosine."

Trigonometric addition formulas for sine and cosine

$$\begin{cases} \cos(\alpha + \beta) & = \cos\alpha\cos\beta - \sin\alpha\sin\beta \\ \sin(\alpha + \beta) & = \sin\alpha\cos\beta + \cos\alpha\sin\beta \end{cases}$$

$$\begin{pmatrix} \cos(\alpha+\beta) \\ \sin(\alpha+\beta) \end{pmatrix} = \begin{pmatrix} \cos\beta & -\sin\beta \\ \sin\beta & \cos\beta \end{pmatrix} \begin{pmatrix} \cos\alpha \\ \sin\alpha \end{pmatrix}$$

Tetra "But this... Wait... *Why?*"

Ms. Mizutani "The library is *closed!*"

Once again Ms. Mizutani's announcement put an end to our math talk for the day. It was time for us to head home, and spend some time thinking alone.

"Or is perceiving a form seeing?"

Problems for Chapter 5

Problem 5-1 (Addition formula)

Use calculations to show that the addtion formula

$$\sin(\alpha + \beta) = \sin \alpha \cos \beta + \cos \alpha \sin \beta$$

holds when $\alpha = 30°$ and $\beta = 60°$.

(Answer on page 242)

Problem 5-2 (Addition formula)

Find the value for $\sin 75°$.

(Answer on page 243)

Problem 5-3 (Addition formula)

Rewrite $\sin 4\theta$ in terms of $\sin \theta$ and $\cos \theta$.

(Answer on page 244)

Epilogue

One day, in a quiet math department storeroom . . .

Girl   "Whoa, there's so much cool stuff in here!"

Teacher   "Yeah, it's fun to poke around."

Girl   "What's this?"

      The girl picks up an old handout.

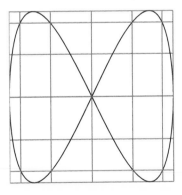

Teacher   "What do you think it is?"

Girl   "A Lissajous curve?"

Teacher   "It is indeed. Or you can think of it as this shape, seen
           from the side."

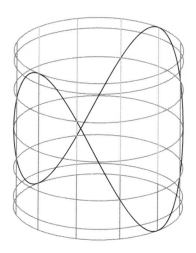

Girl   "Looks like a string wrapped around a cylinder."

Teacher   "Could be a string, could be a sine curve. Might even be
           a floppy circle."

Girl   "What's this? Just a circle?"

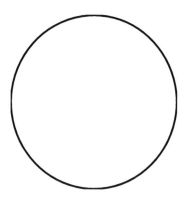

Teacher   "Not quite."

Girl   "Sure looks like a circle."

Teacher   "Actually it's a 96-gon."

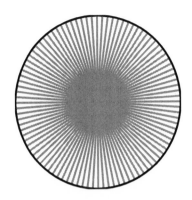

Girl   "Well that's practically a circle."

Teacher   "Archimedes would agree with you. This is the shape he
           used to approximate pi."

Girl   "Using a graph like this?"

Teacher   "No, using calculations."

Girl   "What's this?"

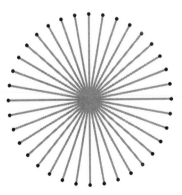

Teacher   "What do you think it is?"

Girl   "Hmm . . . A 36-gon?"

Teacher   "It would be if you connected the dots, yeah."

Girl   "Right."

Teacher   "If you treat each of the points as (x, y) coordinates, let $r = 1$, $\theta = 10°$, and $n = 0, 1, 2, \ldots, 35$, you can write something like this."

$$\begin{cases} x & = r\cos(n\theta) \\ y & = r\sin(n\theta) \end{cases}$$

Girl   "The 0 through 35 is from the 36 points?"

Teacher   "Right. Actually you can let n be all integers if you like, but even with infinitely many n's, only 36 points will be individually distinguishable. Everything piles up on those points."

Girl   "Huh."

Teacher   "Here's another way to think of it. Use a rotation matrix to rotate the point $(1, 0)$ about the origin. You'll get the same graph by raising the rotation matrix to the n-th power."

$$\begin{pmatrix} x \\ y \end{pmatrix} = r^n \begin{pmatrix} \cos\theta & -\sin\theta \\ \sin\theta & \cos\theta \end{pmatrix}^n \begin{pmatrix} 1 \\ 0 \end{pmatrix}$$

Girl   "What's up with that r^n on the right side?"

Teacher   "It lets you fling the points off into space if you like."

Girl   "What do you mean?"

Teacher   "If $r = 1$ the points just spin around on the circle. But if $r > 1$, you get something like this."

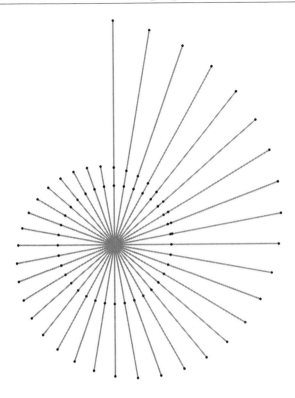

Girl   "Cool! A spiral!"

Teacher   "Yep. A spiral out to infinity as $n \to \infty$."

Girl   "Guess we'll need a bigger piece of paper to graph the whole thing then."

Teacher   "Better to stick to equations on paper, and use your imagination for the graph."

Girl   "You and your equations..."

The girl laughs, waves, and spirals away.

Answers to Problems

> **Problem 1-1 (Finding $\sin \theta$)**
>
> Find the value of $\sin 45°$.

Answer 1-1 (Finding $\sin \theta$)

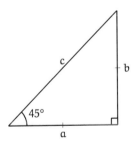

If we consider a right triangle with a $45°$ angle like the one in the diagram, we want to calculate $\frac{b}{c}$. The sum of the interior angles of a triangle is $180°$, so the other angle must be $180° - 90° - 45° = 45°$. We thus have an isosceles right triangle with $a = b$. From the Pythagorean theorem the relation between the side lengths is

$$a^2 + b^2 = c^2,$$

but since $a = b$ we can rewrite this as

$$b^2 + b^2 = c^2.$$

In other words, we have that

$$2b^2 = c^2.$$

We know that $b > 0$ and $c > 0$, so we can divide both sides of this equation by $2c^2$ and take the square root of the result, giving

$$\frac{b}{c} = \frac{1}{\sqrt{2}}.$$

Multiplying the numerator and denominator of the fraction on the right side of this equation by $\sqrt{2}$, we get

$$\frac{b}{c} = \frac{\sqrt{2}}{2},$$

so we obtain $\sin 45° = \frac{\sqrt{2}}{2}$.

Answer: $\sin 45° = \dfrac{\sqrt{2}}{2}$

Note: It is not necessarily incorrect to leave the answer as $\sin 45° = \frac{1}{\sqrt{2}}$, but when performing calculations that use $\sqrt{2} = 1.41421356\cdots$ by hand, $\frac{\sqrt{2}}{2}$ is easier to work out than $\frac{1}{\sqrt{2}}$. For this reason, it has become common practice to remove irrational numbers from denominators, so that fractions can be presented in a standard form. Converting fractions like $\frac{1}{\sqrt{2}}$ into ones like $\frac{\sqrt{2}}{2}$ is called 'rationalizing the denominator.'

Problem 1-2 (Finding θ from $\sin \theta$)

Find all possible values for θ in the range $0° \leqslant \theta \leqslant 360°$ where $\sin \theta = \frac{1}{2}$.

Answer 1-2 (Finding θ from sin θ)

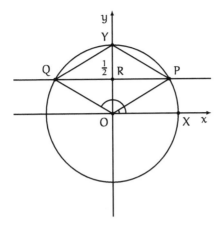

Let the point $(1, 0)$ be point X and let point $(1, 0)$ be point Y, as in the figure. Furthermore, let points P and Q be the points of intersection between a unit circle centered on the origin and the line $y = \frac{1}{2}$. We need to find the angles $\angle XOP$ and $\angle XOQ$. (For convenience, we will assume that $\angle XOP < \angle XOQ$.)

Letting point R be the point $(0, \frac{1}{2})$, $\triangle PRY$ and $\triangle PRO$ are congruent. We know this because they share the side $\overline{PR}$, $\overline{RY} = \overline{RO} = \frac{1}{2}$, and $\angle PRY$, $\angle PRO$ are both right angles.

Since $\triangle PRY$ and $\triangle PRO$ are congruent, $\overline{YP} = \overline{OP}$. Also, $\overline{OP}$ and $\overline{OY}$ are both radii of a unit circle, so $\overline{OP} = \overline{OY}$, and thus $\overline{YP} = \overline{OP} = \overline{OY}$. In other words, $\triangle POY$ is an equilateral triangle.

Since $\triangle POY$ is an equilateral triangle, the measure of $\angle POY$ must be $60°$, and so $\angle XOP$ is $90° - 60° = 30°$.

By a similar procedure we can show that $\triangle YOQ$, too, is an equilateral triangle, so the measure of $\angle XOQ$ must be $90° + 60° = 150°$.

The angles for θ we are looking for are therefore $30°$ and $150°$.

Answer: $\theta = \{30°, 150°\}$

Problem 1-3 (Finding $\cos\theta$)

Find the value of $\cos 0°$.

Answer 1-3 (Finding $\cos\theta$)

Letting point P be the point $(1, 0)$ on a unit circle centered on the origin, $\cos 0°$ will be the x-coordinate of point P. Therefore, $\cos 0° = 1$.

Answer: $\cos 0° = 1$

Problem 1-4 (Finding θ from $\cos\theta$)

Find all possible values for θ in the range $0° \leqslant \theta \leqslant 360°$ where $\cos\theta = \frac{1}{2}$.

Answer 1-4 (Finding θ from $\cos\theta$)

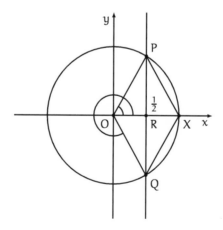

Let point X be the point $(1, 0)$, as in the diagram. Furthermore, let points P and Q be the points of intersection between a unit circle centered on the origin and the line $x = \frac{1}{2}$. We need to find the angles $\angle XOP$ and $\angle XOQ$. (For convenience, we will assume that $\angle XOP < \angle XOQ$.)

Letting point R be the point $(\frac{1}{2}, 0)$, $\triangle PRX$ and $\triangle PRO$ are congruent. We know this because they share the side $\overline{PR}$, $\overline{RY} = \overline{RO} = \frac{1}{2}$, and $\angle PRX$, $\angle PRO$ are both right angles.

Since $\triangle PRX$ and $\triangle PRO$ are congruent, $\overline{XP} = \overline{OP}$. Also, $\overline{OP}$ and $\overline{OX}$ are both radii of a unit circle, so $\overline{OP} = \overline{OX}$, and thus $\overline{XP} = \overline{OP} = \overline{OX}$. In other words, $\triangle POX$ is an equilateral triangle.

Since $\triangle POX$ is an equilateral triangle, the measure of $\angle XOP$ must be $60°$.

By a similar procedure we can show that $\triangle XOQ$, too, is an equilateral triangle, so the measure of $\angle XOQ$ must be $360° - 60° = 300°$.

The angles for θ we are looking for are therefore $60°$ and $300°$.

$$\text{Answer: } \theta = \{60°, 300°\}$$

Problem 1-5 (Graphing $x = \cos \theta$**)**

Draw a graph of $x = \cos \theta$ for values of θ in the range $0° \leqslant \theta \leqslant 360°$. In the graph, use values of θ for the horizontal axis, and values of x for the vertical axis.

Answer 1-5 (Graphing $x = \cos \theta$**)**

The following is a graph of $x = \cos \theta$:

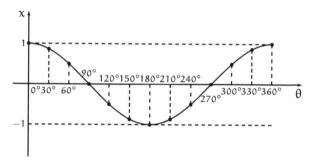

A graph of $x = \cos \theta$

Compare this with the following graph of $y = \sin \theta$:

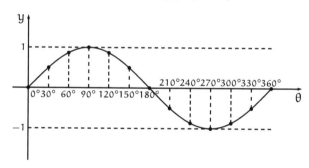

A graph of $y = \sin \theta$

The following graphs show the relation between those of $x = \cos \theta$ and $y = \sin \theta$ on a unit circle. Please examine these closely, and confirm for yourself that the x-coordinate of a point on the unit circle is $\cos \theta$, and the y-coordinate is $\sin \theta$.

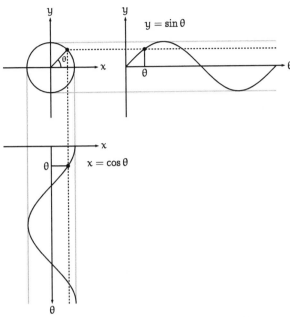

Graphs of $x = \cos\theta$ **and** $y = \sin\theta$

Answers to Chapter 2 Problems

Problem 2-1 (Sine and cosine)

Let's compare values of $\cos\theta$ and $\sin\theta$ with 0.
In the table below,

- if the value is greater than zero 0, write a "$+$,"

- if the value equals 0, write a "0," and

- if the value is less than 0 write a "$-$."

θ	$0°$	$30°$	$60°$	$90°$	$120°$	$150°$
$\cos\theta$	$+$					
$\sin\theta$	0					

θ	$180°$	$210°$	$240°$	$270°$	$300°$	$330°$
$\cos\theta$	$-$					
$\sin\theta$	0					

Answer 2-1 (Sine and cosine)

The completed table is as follows:

θ	$0°$	$30°$	$60°$	$90°$	$120°$	$150°$
$\cos\theta$	$+$	$+$	$+$	0	$-$	$-$
$\sin\theta$	0	$+$	$+$	$+$	$+$	$+$

θ	$180°$	$210°$	$240°$	$270°$	$300°$	$330°$
$\cos\theta$	$-$	$-$	$-$	0	$+$	$+$
$\sin\theta$	0	$-$	$-$	$-$	$-$	$-$

This is easier to visualize as a point traveling along a unit circle, and asking yourself

- if the x-coordinate $(\cos\theta)$ is to the left or right of the y-axis, and

- if the y-coordinate $(\sin\theta)$ is above or below the x-axis.

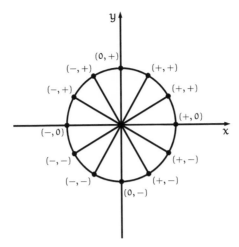

Another approach is to look at graphs of $x = \cos\theta$ and $y = \sin\theta$, and seeing if the values are above or below the θ-axis.

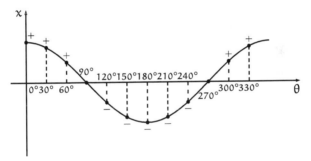

The graph of $x = \cos\theta$

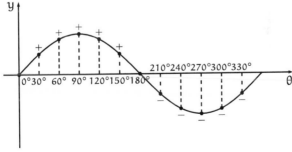

The graph of $y = \sin\theta$

Problem 2-2 (Lissajous curves)

Use the Lissajous graph template on p. 80 to graph point (x, y) for θ in the range $0° \leqslant \theta < 360°$, as follows:

(1) Point $(x, y) = (\cos(\theta + 30°), \sin(\theta + 30°))$

(2) Point $(x, y) = (\cos\theta, \sin(\theta - 30°))$

(3) Point $(x, y) = (\cos(\theta + 30°), \sin\theta)$

Answer 2-2 (Lissajous curves)

The point in (1) describes the curve in the graph below. This is the same as the curve described by point $(x, y) = (\cos\theta, \sin\theta)$.

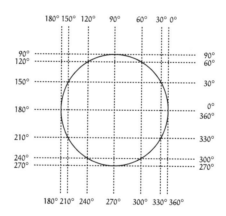

(1) The curve described by
point $(x, y) = (\cos(\theta + 30°), \sin(\theta + 30°))$

The point in (2) describes the curve in the graph below.

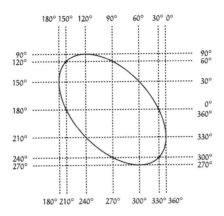

(2) The curve described by point $(x, y) = (\cos\theta, \sin(\theta - 30°))$

The point in (3) describes the curve in the graph below. This is the same curve as that in part (2).

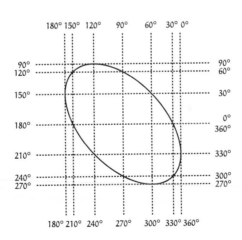

(3) The curve described by point $(x, y) = (\cos(\theta + 30°), \sin\theta)$

ANSWERS TO CHAPTER 3 PROBLEMS

Problem 3-1 (Rotating points)

- Taking the origin $(0, 0)$ as the center of rotation,

- and θ as the angle of rotation,

- and $(1, 0)$ as the starting point,

find the point (x, y) following the rotation.

Answer 3-1 (Rotating points)

You can answer this in the same way Tetra answered Problem 1 on page 112.

$$\text{Answer: } (x, y) = (\cos \theta, \sin \theta)$$

Problem 3-2 (Rotating points)

- Taking the origin $(0, 0)$ as the center of rotation,

- and θ as the angle of rotation,

- and $(0, 1)$ as the starting point,

find the point (x, y) following the rotation.

Answer 3-2 (Rotating points)

You can answer this in the same way Tetra answered Problem 2 on page 115.

$$\text{Answer: } (x, y) = (-\sin \theta, \cos \theta)$$

Problem 3-3 (Rotating points)

- Taking the origin $(0, 0)$ as the center of rotation,

- and θ as the angle of rotation,

- and $(1, 1)$ as the starting point,

find the point (x, y) following the rotation.

Answer 3-3 (Rotating points)

You can answer this by adding respective coordinates from the answers to Problem 3-1 and Problem 3-2.

$$(x, y) = (\cos \theta, \sin \theta) + (-\sin \theta, \cos \theta)$$
$$= (\cos \theta - \sin \theta, \sin \theta + \cos \theta)$$

Answer: $(x, y) = (\cos \theta - \sin \theta, \sin \theta + \cos \theta)$

Problem 3-4 (Rotating points)

- Taking the origin $(0, 0)$ as the center of rotation,

- and θ as the angle of rotation,

- and (a, b) as the starting point,

find the point (x, y) following the rotation.

Answer 3-4 (Rotating points)

This is the same as the answer to the problem on page 120.

Answer: $(x, y) = (a \cos \theta - b \sin \theta, a \sin \theta + b \cos \theta)$

ANSWERS TO CHAPTER 4 PROBLEMS

Problem 4-1 (Measuring pi)

Think of a way to estimate pi using a ruler. For example, measure the circumference and diameter of some cicular object. Call the circumference ℓ and the diameter a. How can you use this information to estimate pi?

Answer 4-1 (Measuring pi)

Since
$$\text{diameter} \times \text{pi} = \text{circumference},$$
after measuring the circumference ℓ and diameter a, pi will be approximately
$$\frac{\ell}{a} \quad (\ell \div a).$$

$$\text{Answer: } \frac{\ell}{a} \quad (\ell \div a)$$

Problem 4-2 (Weighing pi)

Think of a way to estimate pi using a scale. For example, cut a circle of radius a out of heavy construction paper, and weigh it using a precise digital kitchen scale. Next, cut out a square with side length a, and weigh that. Let the weight of the circle be x grams, and that of the square be y grams. How can you use this information to estimate pi?

Answer 4-2 (Weighing pi)

You can estimate pi by taking advantage of the fact that weight is proportional to surface area. Since
$$\frac{\text{area of a circle}}{\text{area of a square}} = \frac{\pi a^2}{a^2} = \pi,$$

an approximate value of pi will be

$$\frac{x}{y} \quad (x \div y)$$

(the weight of the circle divided by the weight of the square).

Answer: $\dfrac{x}{y} \quad (x \div y)$

Answers to Chapter 5 Problems

Problem 5-1 (Addition formula)

Use calculations to show that the addtion formula

$$\sin(\alpha + \beta) = \sin\alpha\cos\beta + \cos\alpha\sin\beta$$

holds when $\alpha = 30°$ and $\beta = 60°$.

Answer 5-1 (Addition formula)

We have already seen some specific values for sin and cos, as follows (see p. 40):

$$\sin(30° + 60°) = \sin 90°$$
$$= 1$$
$$\sin 30° = \frac{1}{2}$$
$$\sin 60° = \frac{\sqrt{3}}{2}$$
$$\cos 30° = \frac{\sqrt{3}}{2}$$
$$\cos 60° = \frac{1}{2}$$

We can therefore calculate the left and right sides of the addition formula as

$$\text{left side} = \sin(\alpha + \beta)$$
$$= \sin(30° + 60°) \qquad \text{because } \alpha = 30°, \beta = 60°$$
$$= \sin 90° \qquad \text{added}$$
$$= 1, \quad \text{and}$$
$$\text{right side} = \sin \alpha \cos \beta + \cos \alpha \sin \beta$$
$$= \sin 30° \cos 60° + \cos 30° \sin 60° \quad \text{because } \alpha = 30°, \beta = 60°$$
$$= \frac{1}{2} \cdot \frac{1}{2} + \frac{\sqrt{3}}{2} \cdot \frac{\sqrt{3}}{2}$$
$$= \frac{1}{4} + \frac{3}{4}$$
$$= 1.$$

The left and right sides are equal, so we have shown that

$$\sin(\alpha + \beta) = \sin \alpha \cos \beta + \cos \alpha \sin \beta.$$

Problem 5-2 (Addition formula)

Find the value for $\sin 75°$.

Answer 5-2 (Addition formula)

We can solve this using the addition formula for the sine function, taking advantage of the fact that $75° = 45° + 30°$. We will use the following values (see p. 40):

$$\sin 45° = \frac{\sqrt{2}}{2}$$

$$\sin 30° = \frac{1}{2}$$

$$\cos 45° = \frac{\sqrt{2}}{2}$$

$$\cos 30° = \frac{\sqrt{3}}{2}$$

The calculation is as follows:

$$
\begin{aligned}
\sin 75° &= \sin(45° + 30°) \\
&= \sin 45° \cos 30° + \cos 45° \sin 30° \\
&= \frac{\sqrt{2}}{2} \cdot \frac{\sqrt{3}}{2} + \frac{\sqrt{2}}{2} \cdot \frac{1}{2} \\
&= \frac{\sqrt{2}\sqrt{3}}{4} + \frac{\sqrt{2}}{4} \\
&= \frac{\sqrt{6} + \sqrt{2}}{4}
\end{aligned}
$$

Answer: $\sin 75° = \dfrac{\sqrt{6} + \sqrt{2}}{4}$

Problem 5-3 (Addition formula)

Rewrite $\sin 4\theta$ in terms of $\sin \theta$ and $\cos \theta$.

Answer 5-3 (Addition formula)

We can do this using the trigonometric addition formulas (see p. 217). To do so, we first represent $\sin 2\theta$ and $\cos 2\theta$ in terms of $\cos \theta$ and $\sin \theta$, respectively, then use the results to represent $\sin 4\theta$.

$$\sin 2\theta = \sin\theta\cos\theta + \cos\theta\sin\theta \qquad \text{from the addition formula}$$
$$= \sin\theta\cos\theta + \sin\theta\cos\theta \qquad \text{swap order of product}$$
$$= 2\sin\theta\cos\theta$$
$$\cos 2\theta = \cos\theta\cos\theta - \sin\theta\sin\theta \qquad \text{from the addition formula}$$
$$= \cos^2\theta - \sin^2\theta$$

From the above, we have obtained the double angle formulas

$$\begin{cases} \sin 2\theta & = 2\sin\theta\cos\theta \\ \cos 2\theta & = \cos^2\theta - \sin^2\theta. \end{cases}$$

We can use these to find $\sin 4\theta$, as follows:

$$\sin 4\theta = 2\sin 2\theta\cos 2\theta \qquad \begin{array}{l}\text{double angle formula,} \\ \text{letting } 4\theta = 2(2\theta)\end{array}$$
$$= 2(2\sin\theta\cos\theta)(\cos^2\theta - \sin^2\theta) \qquad \text{double angle formula, again}$$
$$= 4\sin\theta\cos\theta(\cos^2\theta - \sin^2\theta) \qquad \text{remove first parentheses}$$

Answer: $\sin 4\theta = 4\sin\theta\cos\theta(\cos^2\theta - \sin^2\theta)$

You can also expand this as $\sin 4\theta = 4\sin\theta\cos^3\theta - 4\cos\theta\sin^3\theta$.

Addendum: There are several other ways of writing the double angle formula for cosine, taking advantage of the equation $\cos^2\theta + \sin^2\theta = 1$.

Double angle formulas for cosine

$$\cos 2\theta = \begin{cases} \cos^2\theta - \sin^2\theta \\ 1 - 2\sin^2\theta \\ 2\cos^2\theta - 1 \end{cases}$$

Using these, there are several other ways of representing $\sin 4\theta$. Each of the following are therefore also correct:

$$\sin 4\theta = \begin{cases} 4\sin\theta\cos\theta(\cos^2\theta - \sin^2\theta) & = 4\sin\theta\cos^3\theta - 4\cos\theta\sin^3\theta \\ 4\sin\theta\cos\theta(1 - 2\sin^2\theta) & = 4\sin\theta\cos\theta - 8\cos\theta\sin^3\theta \\ 4\sin\theta\cos\theta(2\cos^2\theta - 1) & = 8\sin\theta\cos^3\theta - 4\cos\theta\sin\theta \end{cases}$$

More Problems

In this section are some additional, slightly different problems for those who want to think more about the topics discussed in the conversations in this book. The answers won't be given here, and there won't necessarily be only one correct solution.

I hope you'll take your time and enjoy these problems, either alone or with a friend.

EXTRA CHAPTER 1 PROBLEMS

Extra credit 1-X1 (Finding $\cos^2\theta + \sin^2\theta$)

It is common in mathematics to abbreviate $(\cos\theta)^2$ as $\cos^2\theta$, and $(\sin\theta)^2$ as $\sin^2\theta$. Try finding the following values:

(a) $\cos^2 0° + \sin^2 0°$

(b) $\cos^2 30° + \sin^2 30°$

(c) $\cos^2 45° + \sin^2 45°$

(d) $\cos^2 60° + \sin^2 60°$

(e) $\cos^2 90° + \sin^2 90°$

While you're at it, try using the definitions of $\cos\theta$ and $\sin\theta$ to show that
$$\cos^2\theta + \sin^2\theta = 1.$$

Extra credit 1-X2 (Negative angles)

Try investigating $\sin\theta$ and $\cos\theta$ when θ is negative, in other words when $\theta < 0°$. For example, what would be the values of $\sin(-30°)$ and $\cos(-90°)$?

Extra credit 1-X3 (Large angles)

Try investigating $\sin\theta$ and $\cos\theta$ when θ is larger than $360°$, in other words when $\theta > 360°$. For example, what would be the values of $\sin(390°)$ and $\cos(450°)$?

Extra credit 1-X4 (cos and sin)

Find all values of θ in the range $0° \leqslant \theta \leqslant 360°$ such that

$$\cos \theta = \sin \theta$$

What are the values when the restriction on θ is removed?

EXTRA CHAPTER 2 PROBLEMS

Extra credit 2-X1 (Cosine and sine)

Letting α and β take values $0°, 30°, 60°, \ldots, 330°$, find all pairs (α, β) such that

$$\cos \alpha = \sin \beta$$

Try doing this using the Lissajous graph paper on page 80.

Extra credit 2-X2 (Reverse Lissajous curves)

Looking at the curves described by points $(x, y) = (\cos \theta, \sin(2\theta + \alpha))$ (p. 77) and points $(x, y) = (\cos 2\theta, \sin(3\theta + \alpha))$ (p. 78), try to find curves that exactly overlay these when flipped top-to-bottom. What's the relation between respective α values in such curves? What about for curves that are flipped left-to-right?

Extra credit 2-X3 (Lissajous curves and bounces)

Looking at the curves described by points $(x, y) = (\cos \theta, \sin(2\theta + \alpha))$ (p. 77) and points $(x, y) = (\cos 2\theta, \sin(3\theta + \alpha))$ (p. 78), investigate how many up–down and left–right 'bounces' the curve makes. Is there some regularity in the number of bounces?

EXTRA CHAPTER 3 PROBLEMS

Extra credit 3-X1 (Specific angles)

The discussion in Chapter 3 used θ as the angle of rotation. Try finding where the point ends up using the specific values $\theta = 0°, 30°, 45°, 60°, 90°$.

Extra credit 3-X2 (Moving points)

The discussion in Chapter 3 was related to where a point (a, b) ends up after a rotation. What other ways can you think of for moving a point? Can you represent those as equations?

Extra credit 3-X3 (Drawing circles)

Let r be some real number greater than 0. Where does a point $(r, 0)$ end up after rotating by an angle θ around the origin $(0, 0)$? While you're at it, try deriving the equation

$$x^2 + y^2 = r^2,$$

which describes a circle of radius r about the origin.

Extra credit 3-X4 (Questions)

Two of the questions that the narrator and Tetra discussed were

- What are you looking for? and

- What information have you been given?

These seem to be very obvious questions to ask. Why is it that such obvious questions can be so effective in problem solving?

Extra Chapter 4 Problems

Extra credit 4-X1 (Counting pi)

In Chapter 4 (p. 144), the narrator and Yuri used a circle with radius 50 to determine that

$$3.0544 < \pi < 3.1952.$$

Try repeating their effort on your own. How big would you need to make the circle to determine that pi is $3.14\cdots$?

Extra credit 4-X2 (Figures that are almost circles)

Try using the surface area of a figure that is almost a circle to estimate pi. For example, what do you get if you divide a square into 3×3 equal parts, and use the resulting octagon? (See the diagram below.)

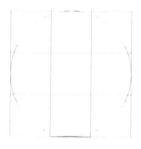

Note: The suggested solution is from the ancient Egyptian Rhind Mathematical Papyrus.

Extra credit 4-X3 (Counting pi)

If, like Yuri, you tried to draw a circle of radius 50 and count the squares, you would probably make some mistakes—it can be hard to tell if a square really is inside the circle, or if it meets it at a corner. Look carefully at the diagram on page 142 and see if you can spot some of the errors that Yuri made. How can you decide for sure if a square is inside the circle or not?

EXTRA CHAPTER 5 PROBLEMS

Extra credit 5-X1 (Inverse rotations)

Chapter 5 showed $\sin(\alpha+\beta)$ represented in terms of four values, $\sin\alpha, \cos\alpha, \sin\beta$ and $\cos\beta$. Try using the same four values to represent $\sin(\alpha - \beta)$.

Extra credit 5-X2 (Another addition formula)

Chapter 5 used a circle to find the addition formula for sine, namely,
$$\sin(\alpha + \beta) = \sin\alpha\cos\beta + \cos\alpha\sin\beta.$$

Use a similar approach to find the addition formula for cosine, which is
$$\cos(\alpha + \beta) = \cos\alpha\cos\beta - \sin\alpha\sin\beta.$$

Extra credit 5-X3 (Generalizing the double angle formulas)

The answer to problem 5-3 (p. 244) used $\sin\theta$ and $\cos\theta$ to represent $\sin 2\theta$ and $\sin 4\theta$. Try using $\sin\theta$ and $\cos\theta$ to represent $\sin 3\theta$ and $\sin 5\theta$.

Extra credit 5-X4 (The double angle formulas and Lissajous curves)

One of the Lissajous curves presented in Chapter 2 (below) looks very much like a parabola.

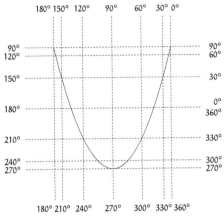

The curve described by
points $(x, y) = (\cos \theta, \sin(2\theta + 90°))$

Use the following two equations to determine if the curve really is a parabola:

$$\sin(\alpha + 90°) = \cos \alpha \qquad \text{relation between sine and cosine}$$
$$\cos 2\beta = 2\cos^2 \beta - 1 \qquad \text{double angle formula}$$

Afterword

Thank you for reading this book. I hope you enjoyed it.

This book is a rearrangement of ten mathematical conversations I posted on the website *Cakes* as a serial feature called "Math Girls: Secret Notebooks." This is a series of fun conversations about fundamental mathematical concepts between four fictional characters: a junior high school student named Yuri, and three high school students, Tetra, Miruka, and the narrator. These are the main characters from *Math Girls*, a separate series of "mathematical romance" novels in which they tackle challenging topics from many areas of mathematics. I hope that once you're comfortable with the content in this series, you'll take on *Math Girls* as well.

As with the *Math Girls* series, this book was produced using LATEX 2_ε and the AMS Euler font. I would like to thank Haruhiko Okumura for his book *Introduction to Creating Beautiful Documents with LATEX 2_ε*, which was an invaluable aid during layout. I created the diagrams using OmniGraffle by The Omni Group and the TikZ graphics package for LATEX. I also used the elementary mathematics handout macro *emath* by Kazuhiro Okuma (a.k.a. tDB), for which I am very grateful.

I would also like to thank the following persons for proofreading my drafts and giving me invaluable feedback, as well as those who did so anonymously. Of course, any errors remaining in the book are solely the responsibility of the author.

Ryo Akazawa, Tatsuya Igarashi, Tetsuya Ishiu, Ryuta Ishimoto, Kazuhiro Inaba, Ryuhei Uehara, Yoichi Uchida, Kento Onishi, Midori Kawakami, Iwao Kimura, Jun Kudo, Kazuhiro Kezuka, Kayo Kotaki, Akiko Sakaguchi, Hayaka Nishihara, Hiroaki Hanada, Aya Hayashi, Izumi Hara, Kasumi Hirai, Hiroshi Fujita, Yutori Bonten (Medaka College), Masahide Maehara, Nami Masuda, Atsushi Matsuura, Kiyoshi Miyake, Ken Murai, Kenta Murata (mrkn), Takeshi Yamaguchi

I would like to thank my editor at Softbank Creative, Kimio Nozawa, for his continuous support throughout both the *Math Girls* and *Math Girls Talk About...* series.

I thank Sadaaki Kato, of *Cakes*.

I thank all my readers, for the support they've given my writing.

I thank my dearest wife and our two sons.

And I thank you, for having read this far. I hope to see you again in the next book in this series.

Hiroshi Yuki

March, 2014

http://www.hyuki.com/girl/

Index

Other works by Hiroshi Yuki

(in English)

- *Math Girls*, Bento Books, 2011
- *Math Girls 2: Fermat's Last Theorem*, Bento Books, 2012
- *Math Girls Manga*, Bento Books, 2013
- *Math Girls Talk About Equations & Graphs*, Bento Books, 2014
- *Math Girls Talk About the Integers*, Bento Books, 2014

(in Japanese)

- *The Essence of C Programming*, Softbank, 1993 (revised 1996)
- *C Programming Lessons, Introduction*, Softbank, 1994 (Second edition, 1998)
- *C Programming Lessons, Grammar*, Softbank, 1995
- *An Introduction to CGI with Perl, Basics*, Softbank Publishing, 1998
- *An Introduction to CGI with Perl, Applications*, Softbank Publishing, 1998

- *Java Programming Lessons (Vols. I & II)*, Softbank Publishing, 1999 (revised 2003)

- *Perl Programming Lessons, Basics*, Softbank Publishing, 2001

- *Learning Design Patterns with Java*, Softbank Publishing, 2001 (revised and expanded, 2004)

- *Learning Design Patterns with Java, Multithreading Edition*, Softbank Publishing, 2002

- *Hiroshi Yuki's Perl Quizzes*, Softbank Publishing, 2002

- *Introduction to Cryptography Technology*, Softbank Publishing, 2003

- *Hiroshi Yuki's Introduction to Wikis*, Impress, 2004

- *Math for Programmers*, Softbank Publishing, 2005

- *Java Programming Lessons, Revised and Expanded (Vols. I & II)*, Softbank Creative, 2005

- *Learning Design Patterns with Java, Multithreading Edition, Revised Second Edition*, Softbank Creative, 2006

- *Revised C Programming Lessons, Introduction*, Softbank Creative, 2006

- *Revised C Programming Lessons, Grammar*, Softbank Creative, 2006

- *Revised Perl Programming Lessons, Basics*, Softbank Creative, 2006

- *Introduction to Refactoring with Java*, Softbank Creative, 2007

- *Math Girls / Fermat's Last Theorem*, Softbank Creative, 2008

- *Revised Introduction to Cryptography Technology*, Softbank Creative, 2008

- *Math Girls Comic (Vols. I & II)*, Media Factory, 2009

- *Math Girls / Gödel's Incompleteness Theorems*, Softbank Creative, 2009

- *Math Girls / Randomized Algorithms*, Softbank Creative, 2011

- *Math Girls / Galois Theory*, Softbank Creative, 2012

- *Java Programming Lessons, Third Edition (Vols. I & II)*, Softbank Creative, 2012

- *Etiquette in Writing Mathematical Statements: Fundamentals*, Chikuma Shobo, 2013

- *Math Girls Secret Notebook / Equations & Graphs*, Softbank Creative, 2013

- *Math Girls Secret Notebook / Let's Play with the Integers*, Softbank Creative, 2013

- *The Birth of Math Girls,* Softbank Creative, 2013

- *Math Girls Secret Notebook / Round Trigonometric Functions*, Softbank Creative, 2014

58306429R00167

Made in the USA
Columbia, SC
19 May 2019